"Jonathan Martin has discovered that 'all the good stuff happens in obscurity.' But it would be a deep problem if this book remained obscure. Drawing on extraordinary insight from Scripture and pastoral practice, Martin illumines what it means to be human. I cannot recommend this book highly enough."

STANLEY HAUERWAS
Gilbert T. Rowe Professor of Theological Ethics, Duke University; named "America's best theologian" by *TIME* magazine

"Jonathan Martin brings a fresh, clear, honest, unbiased approach to ministry that propels you to a new dimension! He has the ability to take all that he has retained in his few years and give us Kingdom food for life. His teachings have encouraged me."

JOHN P. KEE
Pastor and gospel artist

"As I read the manuscript for *Prototype*, I tried to stay objective. Jonathan Martin has been a trusted friend for so long that I was afraid I couldn't allow his book to stand on its own. But three pages in, I forgot who had written the words because the pictures they created and the emotions they evoked laid my heart wide open. Every page showed me new and fresh perspectives on the love of the Father, the person of Jesus, and the work of the Spirit. When I turned the last page, I knew I loved Christ more than when I started. Please give this book your attention!"

CLAYTON KING
President, Crossroads Ministries; teaching pastor at NewSpring Church, South Carolina

"I loved this book! Jonathan Martin is an exceptional teacher who possesses a rare ability to communicate profound insights in profoundly simple ways. Through the use of masterful story-telling, drawn both from Scripture and his own life, Jonathan helps readers wake up to the 'legion' of false identities they have inevitably inherited from our world under the oppression of 'the prince of the power of the air.' This spiritually charged book helps readers begin to experience the fullness of life that is their *true* identity, patterned after our prototype, Jesus Christ. Whether you're a person who has been a believer most of your life or one who is just beginning to wonder what Jesus is all about, you're going to be enriched by the wealth of insights *Prototype* has to offer."

GREG BOYD
Senior Pastor of Woodland Hills Church, St. Paul, Minnesota

"With a winsome blend of personal insight, pop culture references, and serious theological acumen, Jonathan Martin shares his story of growing up as a southern-fried Pentecostal and eventually finding his own voice as an artistic preacher and creative pastor. Most of all, this book is about Jesus, our proto-type for a new way of being human. We need more of this message!"

BRIAN ZAHND
Lead pastor of Word of Life Church, St. Joseph, Missouri;
author of *Beauty Will Save the World*

"*Prototype* reaches out to the millennial generation with a dynamic yet profound application of the love of God demon-strated though the life of Jesus. It is with the utmost confidence that I wholeheartedly endorse this book and recommend it to every minister and believer."

DR. MARK L. WILLIAMS
General Overseer, Church of God International Offices,
Cleveland, Tennessee

PROTOTYPE

WHAT HAPPENS

WHEN YOU DISCOVER

YOU'RE MORE LIKE **JESUS**

THAN YOU THINK?

prototype

jonathan martin

TYNDALE
MOMENTUM

AN IMPRINT OF TYNDALE HOUSE PUBLISHERS, INC.

Visit Tyndale online at www.tyndale.com.

Visit Tyndale Momentum online at www.tyndalemomentum.com.

TYNDALE is a registered trademark of Tyndale House Publishers, Inc. *Tyndale Momentum* and the Tyndale Momentum logo are trademarks of Tyndale House Publishers, Inc. Tyndale Momentum is an imprint of Tyndale House Publishers, Inc.

Prototype: What Happens When You Discover You're More Like Jesus Than You Think?

Designed by Dean H. Renninger

Edited by Dave Lindstedt

Published in association with the literary agency of D. C. Jacobson & Associates, LLC, an author management company; www.dcjacobson.com.

Though the stories told in this book involve real people and actual events, some names have been changed to protect the privacy of the individuals.

ISBN 978-1-4143-7363-8 (softcover)

Printed in the United States of America

19	18	17	16	15	14	13
7	6	5	4	3	2	1

For Ronald and Lynda Martin

✧ ✧ ✧

table of contents

foreword

You're welcome.

That's what I say anytime I have the privilege of introducing someone to the writings and teachings of Jonathan Martin. Not that I'm any part of the reason he's awesome. But if you were friends with Jonathan, you'd claim credit just for knowing him too. He makes everything and everyone he touches smarter and better by association.

Someone tried to explain to me the other day his opinion that there are only two types of relationships: those meant to *comfort* and those meant to *challenge*. He argued that no relationship can equally serve both purposes; it's either one or the other. He made his case with an annoying degree of dogma.

I nodded politely as he went on and on, but in my mind I was seeing a bizarre and hilarious image of Jonathan Martin body-slamming the guy and then bear-hugging him. I was thinking about how my six-foot-five powerhouse friend is the ultimate exception to this man's theory.

I'll give you an example.

One time, I went to see Jonathan just after he got some terrible news about his church having to move out of their building. I figured he'd be breaking down emotionally, and I was prepared to help him to his feet again, even if I had to sit with him all night. Under the same circumstances, I'd likely be in the fetal position, questioning my calling, hating my life.

Why, then, did he meet me at my car, smiling and waving wildly and hugging me when I pulled into the parking lot? (The parking lot, mind you, of the same building he unexpectedly had to vacate within the next month.)

Furthermore, why did he insist on giving me a full tour of the building, stopping at different rooms along the way to describe in detail the miracles God had worked in the lives of the people?

And how, in the name of love, did the evening end with Jonathan and his wife, Amanda, praying for me, encouraging me, comforting me—when I had come, ostensibly, to comfort them?

It was just one of many times I've experienced the superhuman joy and passion that make Jonathan Martin the exception to most theories and the perfect person to write a book on becoming *fully* human.

Jonathan doesn't just challenge me *or* comfort me. His friendship and ministry comfort me in a way that challenges me—to the very core of who I am. Jonathan knows how to speak words of undiluted challenge that flow from pure streams of compassionate comfort.

That's what makes *Prototype* special. That's why I'm confident it will be one of your favorite books. That's why I'm certain God will use it to change your life.

Jonathan presents riveting truth about our identity in Christ in a way that honestly grapples with the intrinsic tensions and mind-boggling implications of the gospel. And he does it while maintaining a sensitive tone in a conversational atmosphere.

He humanizes the process of change—by illustrating the beauty of Jesus.

Usually, a book is either bulletproofed with truth or laden with grace. But when we become *fully* human in all the ways Jesus was, we discover a path to the heart of God that is big enough for both.

As you're about to discover, Jonathan slashes through false dichotomies like a world-class theological graffiti artist. He has a way of retagging issues that have been labeled *either/or* with a big, bold **AND**. He brings the gospel front and center, aggressively, with a brilliance and beauty that is guaranteed to mark you.

Permanently.

I guess this turned out to be more like a warning than a foreword, didn't it?

I have a feeling that's just the way Jonathan would want it.

So, scratch the part at the beginning where I said *you're welcome.*

It's more like you're about to be plunged into the paradoxical prodigy of Jonathan Martin.

Measured *and* unfiltered.

Searing *and* soothing.

Articulate *and* accessible.

Jonathan has written a book designed to body-slam your presuppositions, bear-hug your insecurities, and shake the contents of your heart with a gentle violence. It's not every day you get to meet David and Goliath and it's the same guy.

You've been warned.

And, you're welcome . . .

Steven Furtick

The business of the church is to "remember" the future. Not merely to remember that there is to be a future, but mysteriously to make the future really present.

HERBERT MCCABE,
LAW, LOVE AND LANGUAGE

✧ ✧ ✧

Sometimes the questions are complicated and the answers are simple.

DR. SEUSS

1
identity

✧ ✧ ✧

The most common form of
despair is not being who you are.
SØREN KIERKEGAARD

Who are you?

If I were to ask you that question straight up, you might respond with some version of your Facebook profile: "Here's where I went to school; these are my favorite movies, books, and bands; I like to fish, hunt, play video games, go scuba diving, and listen to Jay-Z."

But who are you *really*, behind the avatars you've created for yourself? What are you covering up? What are you afraid of? What are you hoping for? Where are you going?

If you're like most people in our society, you live in a perpetual identity crisis—with countless voices competing for your attention, across a dizzying array of platforms, telling you who you are and who you ought to be.

So, who are you?

Forgive me for being so forward. I know we've only just met. I don't mean to be abrupt or intrusive. But if we're going to say anything truthful about becoming more like Jesus, surely we have to tell the truth about ourselves first. I know it's a little premature to be disrobing our souls to one another. On the other hand, if you read books the way most people do—in the bedroom or bathroom or squeezed into an uncomfortably small seat on an overcrowded airplane, shielded by the false privacy of headphones—this is already a pretty intimate thing we're doing. Besides, our lives are too important to remain hidden behind self-protective social graces. So, let's get right to it.

What if it were possible to know your true identity? What if it were possible to hear the name we were given before the foundation of the world? What if it were possible to be so truly and fully alive—so *fully human*—that no matter what happened, you would be able to live without fear?

My name is Legion . . . for we are many

One of the more arresting yet disconcerting encounters in the life of Jesus is recorded in Mark 5, when He meets a man terrorized by demons. According to the text, this was a man who "lived among the tombs" (verse 3). Despite multiple attempts to restrain him, not even chains were able to control his volatile behavior. Night and day he roamed the town, "howling and bruising himself with stones" (verse 5). Upon encountering Jesus, the demons within the man were paralyzed with fear: "What have you to do with me, Jesus, Son of the Most High God? I adjure you by God, do not torment me" (verse 7). When Jesus asks the man, "What is your name?" he responds, "My name is Legion; for we are many" (verse 9).

As products of a modern Western culture, in which we seldom dare to wonder whether there is a greater force of evil in the world beyond the sum of its parts, we might find such a story laughably primitive. Given our advances in medical technology, psychology, and biochemistry, and as able as we are to live our lives in relative isolation from the realities of evil, perhaps we feel too sophisticated to take the idea of demons seriously. And yet the plight of the Gerasene demoniac has never been more relevant than in the twenty-first century.

One description of Satan in the New Testament refers to him as "the prince of the power of the air" (Ephesians 2:2, ESV). What a provocative image of evil in an age in which wireless technology has allowed us to be "connected" wherever we are, even as we're hopelessly disconnected from our identity as God's beloved children. "Living among the tombs" seems an apt description of the time we spend in the earbud-enhanced privacy of our own alternate realities, where constant access to technology drives us apart even when we're together. Research has shown that our dependence on technology is changing our brains—and, by most accounts, not for the better.[1] In our day and age, we don't have to believe in demons to be given over to despair and distraction. We simply have to go wireless.

We are subjected to a thousand different voices competing for our attention. We present images of our lives through Facebook, Twitter, or other alternate realities, that are perhaps more reflective of who we want to be than of who we really are.[2] It's so easy to manipulate our "identity" to suit the differing expectations of our home, school, work, religious, and social communities. Never before have we had so many forms of communication at our disposal, and yet rarely has our sense of loneliness and alienation been so profound. In an age of relentless self-expression, do we have any idea who we really are?

The question Jesus asks is a frightening one in a world given over to so many voices, so many images, so many screens, so many sounds, so many identities. In those four simple words—"What is your name?"—everything about the half-life of this man is called into question.

Whether or not we believe in the reality of demons, a truthful response to the question for many of us would be, "My name is Legion . . . for we are many." Many voices, many activities, many interests, many influences.

I find it interesting that it wasn't the sight of a tormented man injuring himself with stones that frightened the Gerasene people. Just as in our day, they had become accustomed to all the noise and violence. It wasn't even the spectacle of two thousand hogs running headlong into the

Sea of Galilee. No, it wasn't all the uproar that caught everyone's attention; it was seeing the former demoniac sitting next to Jesus, clothed and in his right mind, that struck fear in their hearts (Mark 5:15).

In a world where self-destructive behavior has become commonplace, the most frightening scenario may not be a global apocalypse. Perhaps the most startling thing to see is someone whom we have come to expect to be as fragmented, fractured, and self-destructive as we are, transformed into the epitome of sanity, peace, and purpose.

We're afraid, not because we would rather see the demonized man continue to harm himself—we're terrified because his transformation raises for us new possibilities for what it means to be human.

Many of Jesus' contemporaries were versed in the evocative poetry of the prophet Isaiah, with his enchanting vision of a future in which "the wolf shall dwell with the lamb, and the leopard shall lie down with the young goat, and the calf and the lion and the fattened calf together; and a little child shall lead them" (Isaiah 11:6, ESV). It's why a song such as John Lennon's "Imagine" continues to resonate—it's lovely to daydream about a world no longer plagued by the threat of famine, violence, war, or death. As long as these visions exist as a distant utopian fantasy, a counterbalance to a good zombie yarn, they don't threaten us—but neither do they really inspire us.

In a world beleaguered by famine, violence, war, and death, it is far more shocking to see other people who were once as haunted as we are no longer playing by the old rules. In a society in which it is more the norm than the exception for people to have conflicting centers of value and meaning inside their hearts and minds, it is much scarier to encounter people who are sane. If it is possible for one person to transcend the madness and become something other than he or she once was, then it is possible for all of us. And that means the future is no longer a speculative pipe dream. It means the future is upon us. The future is now.

In the life and ministry of Jesus, we see the wonder and chaos of the future breaking into the present. Before the resurrection of Jesus, the account of the Gerasene demoniac was an awful but beautiful foretaste of a new way to be human. We don't know the man's name—it could have been Bob or Phil or an Aramaic version of Kanye. What we do know is that his name was not Legion. He had a name assigned to him before the foundation of the world, a name he had lost touch with. And then, in the midst of his unending self-destructive behavior, in the midst of his round-the-clock angst, amid the pitiless darkness of the tombs, the power of God broke through and reestablished the man's name, his identity as one created in the image of the Father.

The boy on the bike

Let me tell you about the night I learned my own true name. Like any good Southern tale, this one is equal parts ghost story and tent revival testimony.

I grew up in what Flannery O'Connor called the "Christ-haunted landscape" of the American South, in the parsonage of a Pentecostal preacher. Many of the characters in my youth were as colorful as those who populate O'Connor's fiction.

We lived in the little town of Kannapolis, North Carolina, famous mostly for being the hometown of NASCAR legend Dale Earnhardt. I grew up playing church, holding my own little revival meetings with a full complement of superhero action figures. Superman preached the sermon; Aquaman, Robin, and Wonder Woman sang a trio for the special music; Hawkman got saved; and the Green Lantern got the Holy Ghost.

I was reared on a steady diet of apocalyptic stories—sermons and movies about the end of the world. At church one night, we watched *A Thief in the Night*, a B-movie holdover from the 1970s designed to scare us into following Jesus. The film tells the story of a young girl who comes home after school one day to find her parents missing, presumably taken up in the Rapture to go and be with Jesus. She is left to wander the earth alone during the reign of the Antichrist and his goons. It's a pretty dark film, leading up to a climactic scene in which the girl is given the opportunity to either accept "the mark of the beast" and lose her soul forever, or reject the mark and have her head lopped off at the guillotine.

When I was in second grade, my public school teacher showed our class a documentary about Nostradamus, the

sixteenth-century prognosticator who allegedly foretold
modern disasters—from the French Revolution to the rise
and fall of Adolf Hitler to the Kennedy assassination.
Against an ominous background, with images of the
Statue of Liberty being destroyed and New York City
going up in a mushroom cloud, the narrator spoke calmly
about the end of the world. According to the filmmakers,
Nostradamus's visions indicated an impending third world
war—no brighter an outlook than that of John the
Revelator, as seen through the lens of "biblical prophecy
experts" such as Hal Lindsey and Jack Van Impe, who had
written bestselling books about the end times. I could
barely sleep many nights that year.

At eight years old, I remember asking my mother if we
would die from radiation if the Russkies dropped a nuclear
bomb on the city of Charlotte. I had enough sense to know
they weren't likely to go after Kannapolis. (Not everybody
loved Dale Earnhardt, but that was no reason to wipe out
our town.) But I thought Charlotte might be just a big
enough target to put us in harm's way. Needless to say,
I was a pretty terrified little kid, prone to anxiety attacks
from the middle of the day to the middle of the night.

The one escape I had from these apocalyptic fantasies was
my blue-and-silver Schwinn bike. During those same years,
I used to ride my bike for countless hours on the cul-de-sac
at the end of our street. Instead of dwelling on the darker
visions of the end of the world, I escaped into the realm of
the truly fantastic—riding in circles for hours and making

up stories I would tell myself out loud. During these rides, I was unencumbered by fear, doubt, or self-consciousness, freely pursuing all the possibilities—and impossibilities—of life, without ever having to leave the neighborhood.

The neighbors probably thought I had some kind of psychosis, muttering to myself while never actually going anywhere. But I didn't care about getting to the end of the street or to another part of town; my little bike was my time machine. Just being on it made me capable of entering a world in which I had pet robots and saved really gorgeous blondes in futuristic jumpsuits from intergalactic danger. I wouldn't have thought of it in these terms back then, but I honestly believe that's where I came to know God. It was so natural to be in His presence that I wasn't even conscious of it.

I hadn't thought about any of that for almost twenty-five years, until one day when I was praying with my friend Jim Driscoll in my office. Far removed from the apocalyptic night terrors of my youth and the fanciful escapes on my bike, I was now leading a growing church, and it had been a very long time since I had even been on a bicycle, much less owned one. But while we were praying, I suddenly felt an "intensity" in the room—that's the best I can describe it—and Jim spoke words over me that I will never forget:

> Jonathan, while I was praying for you, I saw you as a little boy riding your bike. You're riding around in circles, and you are talking to yourself—you are

making up stories out loud. There is so much freedom
and creativity and imagination in you. You are completely free in the presence of God. I believe God is
saying that is exactly who He wants you to become
again. He wants you to be the boy on the bike again.
He wants you to dream and laugh and create and be
with Him the way you were when you rode in circles.

When I heard those words, I wept without restraint. In
twenty-five years, I hadn't told *anyone* about those long-
forgotten days riding my bike and making up stories—not
even my wife, much less Jim. In the very core of my being,
I knew that God was speaking to me. I just didn't know
what to do with it.

Six months later, Amanda and I were on vacation with
her family in Seabrook Island, South Carolina. When we left
for the beach, I was overwhelmed by some difficult situations
in our church and in my personal life. And because I was
constantly tethered to my electronic gadgets—and everything that goes along with being "connected"—I couldn't
find a way to escape.

On our first night at Seabrook Island, I decided to go
for a bike ride. My in-laws had recently bought me a new
bicycle, but I hadn't had the opportunity yet to ride it. It
was around ten o'clock, and because there are no street-
lights on the island, I went looking for a safely lit space to
ride. Some nearby condos had a few lights along the perimeter of their property, and I decided that would do.

As I rode around in the parking lot, I was overcome by a familiar presence—as if suddenly I was no longer alone. It is difficult to describe, but I felt overwhelmed by the intensity of God's love for me. I had not experienced Him quite like that before. Over and over again, I sensed Him reminding me that I was His beloved son—and that He loved me exactly as I was. It was not an out-of-body experience; yet it was as if my bike had become a time machine again—even more vividly than when I was in the second grade. For almost an hour, I was completely unaware of my surroundings or that tears were pouring down my face. When I finally realized that I had become a tearful, snotty, glorious mess, I composed myself and prepared to ride home. It was only then that Jim's words came back to me.

Caught up in the moment, I hadn't realized that I had been riding around in a circle for the entire hour. At that point, my weeping gave way to laughter, and I remember thinking, *God, I had no idea you were being quite so literal about this whole boy on the bike thing!* Even though, as a pastor, I had already preached to and counseled many people about how to have a relationship with God, I think it was the first time I had really come to know my own identity in Him.

When was your "boy on a bike" experience?

I don't know if my story sounds too mystical for you, like one more religious leader trying to convince you that he hears from God. But as I've shared my story with friends,

I've discovered there is something elemental, something universal, about the "boy on the bike" experience—a time when we all have felt the most alive, the most awake to God and to the world, unconstrained by fear, doubt, or loneliness. For my friend Tracey, it was times of jumping on a trampoline as a girl. Another friend told me about a vivid, persistent image he saw in his mind's eye of himself as a young boy in a blue zip-up sleeper, brandishing a sword.

When I was on my blue-and-silver Schwinn as a boy, I believe I was aware of God in some primal way, though not because I was thinking a lot about Him directly. Mostly I was making up science fiction stories and telling them to myself out loud. But wrapped up in that experience was something essential, vital, visceral about my identity as a child of God.

Whether or not you are a boy on a bike or with a sword, or a girl on a trampoline, odds are there has been a moment in your life when you were filled with a sense of wonder and mystery at something outside of yourself. It doesn't have to be an experience that you felt was "spiritual" or "religious." Simply a time when you were open and free to the world around you, or a time when you had a sense that there was something, or someone, drawing you close. Maybe you can even remember a time when you knew the sensation of being fully known and delighted in.

I believe there was a time in your life, sometime before you succumbed to the constant busyness, noise, and distraction of our world, when you knew something of the loving presence of God. There was a time (perhaps associated with a place) when you knew—or at least suspected—that you were infinitely loved. In other words, I believe you have heard from God, and that you probably know a lot more about hearing from God than you might realize.

What if there is something to that faint suspicion in your heart that there is a force of love and logic at work in the universe, who knows who you are and what you are up to? That sense—however fleeting—that something, or someone, beyond you takes delight in who you are and how you are made? It's easy to dismiss such things as childish fantasy. After all, what did we really know about the world when we were eight? And yet, Jesus did teach that unless we "change and become like children," we will not "enter the kingdom of heaven" (Matthew 18:3). He wasn't saying that we need to be irrational, check our brains at the door, and hang on to naive fairy tales. But I think in a way He calls us back to that moment of wonder and mystery when we encountered God with the innocence of childhood.

The experience of God will always be trans-rational; it goes beyond our capacity to analyze or reason. For all the good things we've gained as we have grown, we've also picked up a lot of baggage that makes it difficult to remember the boy on the bike or the girl on the trampoline. When we were young and innocent, a bike could be a time machine, a trampoline could be a gateway into another dimension—just as a common wardrobe becomes a doorway into another realm of existence in C. S. Lewis's Chronicles of Narnia.

You and I have lived with enough ambiguity and experienced enough pain since our younger days that it seems impossible to go back. But what if it were possible to return to those moments? What if we could go back to being the boy on the bike or the girl on the trampoline? We have more than enough reasons to settle for being older and wiser and weathered and seasoned and smarter—reasons to know better. But isn't there something in your heart that aches to go back and recapture that assurance? Doesn't it seem as if there's something truthful about those experiences that you can't quite shake? What if when you were younger and less encumbered by the expectations and identities that have been assigned to you by so many other voices, you understood deeper things about life and God and the world than you do now? Wouldn't that be worth going back for?

You might identify with the experience of being a boy on a bike or a girl on a trampoline and not associate anything you saw or felt then as "God." That's the beautiful thing about coming to faith. It's not about changing anything in your world—at least not at first. It's about coming to see the world that you already know, but in a new way. It's a new set of lenses and a new language, so that now when you look at the same world, you see something different, and you have a new vocabulary to describe familiar experiences.

It's not even so much about *finding* something new; it's more about *recognition*, about seeing things for the first time as they truly are. It's interesting how people who come to understand God's love for them often describe the feeling as a *homecoming*, even if they can't remember being "home" to begin with. There's a reason for this. Coming awake to God's infinite love can seem so foreign and yet feel as if it's where we've always belonged, because God, in His hovering delight, knows every boy on a bike and every girl on a trampoline. That sense of being known and delighted in stalks human beings the world over, even when we do everything in our power to act as if we do not know love.

What would it mean to believe that you already know something of the inner voice of love?[3] What would it mean to start to listen to that voice? To give in to it? What if you really had a name before the cosmos existed? How would that change your approach to today?

Coming awake to God is nothing to be afraid of. It's not like doing something entirely different from anything you've ever done, or going somewhere you've never been. It's about coming home to who you really are. It's about becoming more yourself—more fully human—than ever.

This book is not about finding religion. It's not a self-help manual. I don't have seven habits or twelve steps to take you anywhere. This is about becoming *awake* to God. And if we become awake to God, we become awake to everything and everyone around us.

There are different ways to recognize God's voice. It may not be clear. It may not be loud. In fact, in my own experience, one of the things that sets apart the voice of God from all the other voices is that it is so often inconspicuous. You have to *listen* for it.

There is a beautiful story in 1 Kings 19 about the prophet Elijah at a time when he is on the run and desperate to encounter God. After he takes refuge in a cave on the side of a mountain, he is told to go outside because the presence of the Lord is about to pass by.

> Then a great and powerful wind tore the mountains apart and shattered the rocks before the Lord, but the Lord was not in the wind. After the wind there was an earthquake, but the Lord was not in the earthquake. After the earthquake came a fire, but the Lord was not in the fire. And after the fire came a gentle whisper. When Elijah heard it, he pulled his cloak over his face and went out and stood at the mouth of the cave. (1 Kings 19:11-13, NIV)

That's my hope for you as you read this book. Regardless of whether you find any of my words to be especially brilliant, poetic, or poignant, I want more than anything for you to hear the gentle whisper of God's voice. And though His voice may sound different to you than it does to me, I'm confident that you will recognize it.

Jesus as our prototype

Ever since that night on the bike at the beach, I've been learning more about who I am and who God is. I still get scared sometimes, and on occasion I'm an absolute wreck. There are plenty of things I don't like about myself and that you probably wouldn't like either. It seems weird to me to be a pastor, because I don't feel like I'm "together" enough—it's one of those "inmates running the asylum" kind of things. But ever since I discovered that I am the boy on the bike, I have learned more and more about what it means to be a beloved child of God. And in the best of moments, I see evidence that this revelation is turning me into somebody else—somebody more like Jesus.

Please understand, there are so many ways in which I am not yet at all like Jesus. But like Jesus, I now know my identity as God's beloved son. Like Jesus, I live with an awareness of God's presence that I didn't have before. Like Jesus, I'm now able to live unafraid of the future, because the future has already come barreling down on me. I'm learning to live more boldly, less fearfully, and less tentatively than I used to. I am more like a man from the future who is fully alive in the present.

As the sinless, only begotten Son of God—fully human and fully divine—Jesus is unique. I don't want to downplay any aspect of His character. But the fact that He could do extraordinary wonders is not what made Him so special. Even more than all the miracles, what set Jesus apart was the deep understanding and trust He had that He was loved by God the Father.

Jesus was so certain of who He was and where He was going that of course He became a threat to the world around Him. He didn't need the affirmation of other people to know His true identity. What could possibly be more futuristic than that? Love made him free to be human in a way that nobody else before Him had been.

Many times in the Old Testament, God refers to human beings as His beloved. But when God called Jesus His beloved, Jesus did something truly remarkable: *He believed Him*. And He lived every moment of His life fully convinced of His identity.

And unlike every other person in human history . . . He never forgot.

The reason Jesus was such a threat to the religious authorities of His time was not that He went around teaching people to be nice to one another. The reason He was such a threat was that He showed us a new way to be human. That's why He ultimately had to be crucified—He was calling others into this new humanity, and it was dangerous for the social order of the day. And not just *His* day, but ours as well.

What if the ultimate goal of everything Jesus said and did was not just to get us to believe certain things about Him, but to *become* like Him? What if it were possible to become fully human in all the ways that Jesus was? What if Jesus were God's prototype for a whole new way of being human?

Because I'm a pastor, you would be right to assume that I think it matters a great deal what we think about Jesus. I'm quite partial to Jesus. I think it makes all the difference in the world to believe in Him. But what's interesting about believing *in* Jesus is that it has a whole lot to do with believing *like* Jesus—believing that you are beloved as a son or daughter of God; believing what God says about you, that you are the boy on the bike or the girl on the trampoline (or whatever your specific identity is), no matter what anyone else calls you.

Having discovered my rightful identity as God's beloved (aka the boy on the bike) has by no means straightened out everything in my life. But it has made my life much simpler. I now understand that knowing who God says we are and following Jesus into this new way of being human will change everything about our lives. The world is not ready for people like us. The world is not ready for a message like this—it is too futuristic. The world runs the way it does because we are people of the present—people with so much to do and so much to be afraid of. When we begin to live like Jesus, people will perceive our peace as an indictment on their violence; they will see our security as an indictment on their insecurity. It is a fearful thing to behold someone who is truly human in all the ways that Jesus said we could be—precisely because we have nothing left to be afraid of. We have already faced the future, so the future is not intimidating to us anymore.

In the coming pages, I want to show you how Jesus

came to be the prototype for this new way of being human. And I want you to discover (or reconnect with) your true self so you can begin the process of becoming more like Him. Though we may see ourselves as liars, dreamers, and misfits, I want to show you how we can unite as beloved children of God—people from the future who are fully alive in the present.

2
beloved

✧ ✧ ✧

I salt my breakfast eggs. All day long I feel created.
I can see the blown dust on the skin of the back of my
hand, the tiny trapezoids of chipped clay, moistened
and breathed alive. There are some created sheep in the
pasture below me, sheep set down here precisely, just
touching their blue shadows hoof to hoof on the grass.
Created gulls pock the air, rip great curved seams in the
settled air: I greet my created meal, amazed.

ANNIE DILLARD, *HOLY THE FIRM*

We were created to be the boy on the bike or the girl on the
trampoline. Because we are formed in the image of God,
we are born with the capacity to dream, to imagine, to play,
to create. The bike and the trampoline are important, you
see, but they're only props. When I was on my bike, my
mind and heart were opened up to see things beyond the
boundaries of reality as I knew it. Those were moments

when my soul opened up wide enough to imagine a different world from the one I'd been given. And my creativity was boundless for envisioning such a world because those were moments when I did not feel fear.

But as we get older, we find more and more reasons to be afraid. As Bruce Springsteen describes with haunting precision in his song "Devils and Dust,"

> *Fear's a powerful thing, baby.*
> *It can turn your heart black you can trust.*
> *It'll take your God-filled soul*
> *And fill it with devils and dust.*[1]

We were conceived in delight and baptized into wonder before we even had a name. There was one who beheld us in our unformed substance, singing over us, delighting in us. Because the enchantment of divine love was there before we were born, it is native to us; we all have a primal desire inside of us to be the object of that delight, to be fully known before a God who celebrates us.

But *fear's a powerful thing, baby. It can turn your heart black you can trust.* And as we live and grow in a world that tells us we're never enough—that we have to prove our worth and demonstrate our value—our souls, which were designed to be filled with God, are filled with devils and dust.

Increasingly, I'm coming to believe that fear is at the heart of all sin and disaffection. Fear that God will not be enough for us; fear that the identity we've been given is somehow incomplete. And we live in a world in which so many people tell us that we have so much to be afraid of. It's how the legion rules us: by manipulating our fears. We are taught to fear rejection, to fear others, to fear germs, to fear the world, to fear death, to fear the future. The forces that the apostle Paul calls "principalities" and "powers"[2] (broad terms that encompass personalities and systems in both the spiritual and natural order) dominate us through our fears. It can be difficult to discern this, because fear usually comes cloaked in the language of responsibility: "Of course you should be afraid of this person/political party/activity. The world is a dangerous place; it only makes sense to be careful."

The more conscious we become of our fears, the more mindful we are to protect ourselves and our hearts. And the more we try to protect ourselves, the less able we are to connect with the boy on the bike or the girl on the trampoline. When we protect ourselves from what we fear, we also undermine our capacity for *wonder*.

The short epistle of 1 John makes a shockingly simple claim: *God is love*. It also tells us that "perfect love casts out fear," and "he who fears has not been made perfect in love" (1 John 4:18, NKJV). The language is so clear and direct that the power of this contrast can easily be lost on us. But let it sink in for a moment: If God is love, and perfect love casts out fear, then fear is the opposite of everything that God is. If perfect love casts out fear, then perfect fear must also cast out love. To put it more starkly, fear casts out God in our lives.

Becoming an adult in our culture is synonymous with being made perfect in fear. The older we get, the more fragile we feel and the more precarious our future seems. The older we get, the more we feel we have something to lose. Imagination, wonder, joy, and creativity become endangered species. One by one, they begin to die off. But by then we're too preoccupied with all that we fear to even notice that it's happening.

It's a bleak picture, I know. And yet, even in the midst of it, we still have moments when we feel called back to a time when we were not yet afraid—a time before we knew the fear of rejection, fear of people, fear of the world, or fear of ourselves. And that primal innocence is still within us. In the words of the late Irish poet John O'Donohue, we're each "still essentially an ex-baby. . . . There is a place in you where you have never been wounded, where there's still a sureness in you, where there's a seamlessness in you, and where there is a confidence and tranquility in you."[3]

Before you learned to be so afraid, there was a part of you that knew you were loved (or at least had a suspicion). Whether you thought of your boy on the bike or girl on the trampoline experience as an encounter with God or not, I believe you were closer to God in those moments than you may realize. For whenever fear is absent, God is not far away. In those moments when we had an imagination big enough for our souls to inhabit, we knew something of what it means to be made in the image of the Creator. After all, the first thing we learn about God in the Genesis account is that He creates. So when we lived in wonder and explored new worlds with our imagination, we were behaving like our Father without even trying.

Nowadays, we are oversaturated by fear and overstimulated by flashing screens and constant noise. Yet every once in a while, we have moments when we are called back to the simpler life of love instead of fear. Those moments occur mostly when we experience true beauty in some form.

When was the last time you stopped long enough to enjoy and appreciate the beauty of nature or music or art? When was the last time you felt truly and deeply loved? Whenever we experience something truly beautiful, it's as if someone is leaving a trail of bread crumbs to the place where we are fully known and fully loved. Our task is to follow the bread crumbs to see where they lead.

The boy in the field

There is only one person who lived every moment consumed by love rather than fear, and that is Jesus of Nazareth. And though there's a lot I want to tell you about Jesus and all the ways in which He is the prototype for a new way of being human, to begin with His life might seem too intimidating—because in so many ways He feels "other" from us. Instead, let's begin with the story of a boy in a field, a boy named David, who grew up in obscurity, in the decidedly unromantic job of tending sheep in the wilderness.

Though the events of David's life are often beyond our wildest imaginings—fighting with lions and bears and giants, chasing down marauding bandits, and being chased by kings—during his formative years he was all but forgotten by his own family (to the extent that his father neglected to summon him when the prophet Samuel came calling). Still, it was during those long days and nights alone in the wilderness that David became well acquainted with the perfect love that casts out fear. And it was during this time that he gradually came to suspect that he was the object of God's delight—not in a narcissistic way, as if the world revolved around him, but with a deep and settled conviction of his belovedness in the eyes of his Creator. This blossoming sense of worth and identity opened up the whole world to him.

Long before anyone knew who he was, David wrote beautiful songs that give us a window into his heart. In fact, we can't fully grasp David's story without understanding his music. Here was a man who not only wrote symphonies, his entire life was a symphony: one long, multifaceted composition full of highs and lows, harmony and dissonance; a life that was complex in all the ways that our lives are complex; a life as big as music itself. The boy in the field followed the music in his soul and the poetry of Creation back to God over and over again. He followed the love he felt back to the source.

Even if we can't quite relate to the epic scope of David's later life, through his music we can see something of what he saw and hear something of what he heard about the perfect love that casts out fear. Even when our lives feel small by comparison, the music of the Psalms enlarges our borders. Even when there is nothing remotely epic about our lives, there are prodigious rumblings in our souls—which is why we need songs big enough to escape into.

No one else in the Hebrew Scriptures demonstrates the grasp of God's unfailing love that David had, but his poetry is never sappy or sentimental. On the contrary, it is full of doubt and pain. In fact, so pervasive are the expressions of suffering and woundedness in the Psalms that 70 percent are classified as psalms of lament or mourning.[4]

David wasn't an optimist; he wasn't looking on the sunny side of life. Even in his most successful years as king, his life wasn't easy. His success never fully eradicated the loneliness and despair he carried within him. In fact, I think we can safely surmise there were many times during David's "glory years" when he wished he could go back to the simplicity of his life in the fields. Yet despite all the challenges, the remarkable thread that runs consistently through David's music and the symphony of his life is the sense that he is God's beloved.

If you want a glimpse into David's soul, read his elegant description of God's love in Psalm 139:1-18:

O LORD, you have searched me and known me.
You know when I sit down and when I rise up;
  you discern my thoughts from far away.

You search out my path and my lying down,
   and are acquainted with all my ways.
Even before a word is on my tongue,
   O LORD, you know it completely.
You hem me in, behind and before,
   and lay your hand upon me.
Such knowledge is too wonderful for me;
   it is so high that I cannot attain it.

Where can I go from your spirit?
   Or where can I flee from your presence?
If I ascend to heaven, you are there;
   if I make my bed in Sheol, you are there.
If I take the wings of the morning
   and settle at the farthest limits of the sea,
even there your hand shall lead me,
   and your right hand shall hold me fast.
If I say, "Surely the darkness shall cover me,
   and the light around me become night,"
even the darkness is not dark to you;
   the night is as bright as the day,
   for darkness is as light to you.

For it was you who formed my inward parts;
   you knit me together in my mother's womb.
I praise you, for I am fearfully and wonderfully made.
   Wonderful are your works;
that I know very well.

My frame was not hidden from you,
when I was being made in secret,
 intricately woven in the depths of the earth.
Your eyes beheld my unformed substance.
In your book were written
 all the days that were formed for me,
 when none of them as yet existed.
How weighty to me are your thoughts, O God!
 How vast is the sum of them!
I try to count them—they are more than the sand;
 I come to the end—I am still with you.

For hours, days, weeks, David contemplated the depth of God's love for him—that he had an identity before the world was made, that God was always thinking of him. What does it mean to not be hidden from the eyes of God even in the womb? What does it say about God that He "beheld [David's] unformed substance"? Alone in the field, far removed in both space and time from the overwhelming voices we contend with every day, David came to a remarkable revelation: *He was loved simply because he existed.*

He tried to imagine a scenario in which he could get beyond the love and delight that stalked him in the fields. Was there a place in the cosmos where he could outrun that presence? If he had wings and flew to the end of the sea, could he get beyond God's love? If he made a bed in the shadowy grave—even then could he escape it?

"I come to the end," he says. "I am still with you."

The remarkable thing is that David lived long enough to test all of this. Later in life, it appears he attempted to outrun God's presence, to use his wings to fly far from His voice. He created such a mess for himself that it seemed he had made a bed for himself in hell (Sheol). Yet even when he got to the end—the end of poetic speech, the end of his own strength, the end of his own goodness—God never left him. Before all the testing and all the wrong turns, somehow David's soul knew that the delight that hovered over him and sang over him, the one from whom the music came, would never leave. And it was that knowledge that set David apart from everybody else.

If it was possible for David to grasp how loved he was, even in the midst of his profound brokenness, surely it is possible for you and me to understand that God loves us, too—and *has* loved us, even back when we were an "unformed substance."

The difference between David and Saul

I don't believe that David was uniquely loved by God— only that he uniquely *grasped* his belovedness. To see the difference that makes, all we have to do is take a cursory look at his counterpart and predecessor, King Saul. Like David, Saul was a king over Israel. And like David, he had powerful experiences of the presence of God—there were moments when God ecstatically seized Saul and spoke through him. Saul, like David, did some terribly wrong things—but he was certainly no worse than David. I'm convinced that the essential difference between David and Saul is that David grasped the love of God in a way that Saul never could (or at least never did). I believe David's years of obscurity enabled him to receive a revelation of his belovedness in a way that Saul never could, amid the legion of voices from which he drew his own fractured sense of identity. Through all the worst moments of David's life, it was his intrinsic grasp of God's love that ultimately set him apart. It turns out that knowing how loved we are by God makes all the difference in the kind of people we will become.

Now, to be fair, I am a Saul sympathizer. As one who stands six foot five, I can relate to Saul, who stood head and shoulders above everyone else. More deeply, though, it has always been difficult for me to understand where exactly Saul went wrong—the language in the texts is enigmatic and raises more questions than it answers. But there is one part of the Saul narrative that seems clear to me now: Saul's ultimate failure was deeply connected to his popularity. The most pronounced characteristic of Saul's early life, compared to David's, was that he was always celebrated by people. He was the people's champion, an attractive man accustomed to the accolades of the crowds. He didn't have a legion of demons, but one of adoring fans who sang about his valor and success.

Oddly enough, the legion who affirmed Saul turn out to be as dangerous as the legion who afflicted the demoniac in Mark's Gospel. When the voices stopped singing for him, we see how addicted Saul was to the praise of the crowd. When David slew Goliath, the people started singing a new song: "Saul has killed his thousands, and David his ten thousands." When this song became the number one hit on iTunes, Saul couldn't handle it. In our vernacular, he was jealous that David had more followers on Twitter than he did.

Fear's a powerful thing, baby. It can turn your heart black you can trust. It'll take your God-filled soul and fill it with devils and dust. Saul became afraid of losing his status, afraid of losing his influence, afraid of David's popularity, afraid of the future. Fear snapped Saul in two, and from that point forward, he went as mad as the man known as Legion.

The music we heard in Psalm 139—the song that says "you are loved because you exist," and "you can't outrun love, no matter how far you go or what you do"—is the very same music that Saul heard whenever David played the harp for him. He had access to a playlist called "beloved" every time David dropped by with his soothing melodies. Like Legion, Saul was a fragmented man, a fractured spirit; but enough of his soul was still intact to be soothed by the music (see 1 Samuel 16:23).

For a time, albeit briefly, the music brought Saul out of his madness. For a few moments, he didn't care who the people celebrated or whether they said he had conquered thousands or tens of thousands. Beauty and music have that effect on us—they are the most personal and intimate of lovers. Music can make us feel as if we are the only ones who exist in the universe. Beauty can so fill us with love and awe and wonder that, like David on the hillside watching over his sheep, all we can conceive of is ourselves and the voice that called us beloved before we even had a name.

We've all had moments when we were so captured by wonder—through music, through art, through the beauty of nature—that it quieted all the other voices. As with Saul, there are moments when we encounter the wonder that reminds us of who we really are and of what we are meant to become. We sense we were meant for something more than a life immersed in the monotonous drone of voices that sometimes affirm us and sometimes reject us. Those voices are much louder; the sense of wonder is much more delicate.

Unfortunately, we are also like Saul in that we can contemplate the possibilities of an unconstrained life for only so long before the song ends, the lights come up, and the poetry is flattened into the taunts of the legion: "You are loved if you are successful; you are loved if you are beautiful; you are loved if you prove yourself." When the music fades away and the wonder subsides, we find ourselves right back in the midst of the legion of voices competing for our attention. In the words of Henri Nouwen, "One of the tragedies of our life is that we keep forgetting who we are."[5]

When we encounter genuine beauty, our souls are stirred. There are moments when art or beauty or nature or music truly move us. But can we trust the wonder to lead us back to our true selves, back to the identity we had before we were born into a world full of heartbreak?

The Holy Ghost iPod shuffle phenomenon

Like many people of my generation, I've spent far too much of my life with headphones on my ears. I have a big, DJ-style pair that I use every day, because I love to be immersed in music—I love songs big enough to swim around in. That's one reason why I've had a lifelong affinity for the Irish rock group U2. I know it's a huge cliché for a thirtysomething pastor to be a massive U2 fan. But I don't care. I was listening to their album *Zooropa* on endless repeat on my boom box long before I cared anything about ministry. They have always spoken the language of my spirit—and thankfully, our communicative God is conversant in all of my dialects. More than once, He has used the music of U2 to touch me and guide me.

There was a particularly dark day several years ago when I was convinced that the life I had built for myself was crumbling around me. I had never felt more hurt or confused. Not knowing what else to do on that Saturday morning, I decided to go to a nearby gym to try to work off some of the tension I felt. As I stepped onto the elliptical machine, I turned on my iPod and set it on "shuffle." (I've always liked that feature because it's like having your own personal radio station—except all the bands are awesome and there are no commercials.)

As I began to work the elliptical machine, the anthem "Beautiful Day" came on. Being a U2 buff, I knew the history of that song: Lead singer Bono once said in an interview that he was inspired by the teaching of Christ that you have to lose your life in order to find it. It's a song about losing everything you held dear, and yet somehow finding that you've gained everything that really counts:

> *Sky falls, you feel like*
> *It's a beautiful day,*
> *Don't let it get away*[6]

As I was listening to the music that day, something inside me broke. I felt a distinct inner confirmation—a virtual witness deep within me—that I was experiencing the truth of that song through my particular circumstances.

> *What you don't have you don't need it now.*
> *What you don't know you can feel it somehow.*[7]

I had felt as if I was going to lose everything, but I was suddenly overwhelmed with the certainty that it was actually the beginning of something new and unspeakably beautiful. I didn't know how to articulate it at the time, but I now believe that the distinct vision of the church we planted in Charlotte was birthed in that moment.

I had heard that song hundreds of times before, but that

time I heard it differently. It was as if something had come to life inside me and was getting out, like the creature that bursts from the chest cavity of the guy in the first Alien movie. With tears running down my face, I felt so silly on that elliptical machine in the middle of a crowded gym on a Saturday morning.

This experience took place over the span of about four minutes. As the song was winding down, I was still overcome, but my emotions were starting to settle—that is, until my iPod, still set on "shuffle" and crammed with thousands of songs to choose from, played a live version of "Beautiful Day" right on the heels of the studio cut. At that point, I really began to weep. It was as if the voice of Love was saying, "In case you didn't recognize me the first time . . ."

There may well be a rational explanation for the timing and sequencing of those songs on my iPod that day, but even if that were true, it wouldn't change or diminish the impact of what I heard. My response was not irrational, but it transcended my capacity for reason. I wasn't just hearing U2 play a rock song, I was hearing an ancient song. I was hearing the music of God's love in the same way I believe David heard it in the field as a boy. It was the wonder that called me back to who I really am, that called me forward to who I am meant to become. That's what music does; that's what wonder does. God uses these things to remind us of who we really are.

When have you felt the wonder?

I first sensed the love that casts out fear when my imagination roamed free as a boy on a bike—though it would be years before I understood what it was all about. Where were you when you first felt that sense of wonder and awe and mystery, that ache of realization that you are fully known? Can you recall a time when you encountered something beautiful deeply present within this splendid wreck of a world, and yet somehow not of it? Something beyond yourself that delighted in who you are and how you were made? Something in you that recognized that there is something out there that sings and dances over your very existence?

This same voice that calls you into the prehistoric past (not the world of dinosaurs, but literally *before history*) also summons you into the future—beyond the person you are today to the person you have yet to become, the new kind of human you are meant to be. Perhaps paradoxically, the voice beckons you backward (to rediscover your true self) until you arrive in the future, at a new way of being human.

In a sense, as with David, the wonder calls us into the past. Not just back to the moment when we were the boy on a bike or the girl on a trampoline; not back to the cradle, or even to the womb; but back even further, to an unformed substance that was known and utterly loved through eyes full of tenderness. The wonder calls us back to a God who hovered over us in delight even before we had fingers or toes or mouths to say or do anything for anyone to approve or disapprove.

The wonder calls us back to the beginning—to the source. In J. R. R. Tolkien's *The Silmarillion*, which provides background and context for his Lord of the Rings trilogy, God is said to have sung the creation into existence. Now, I know that Tolkien didn't write one of the Gospels, but I think he may have tapped into the same kind of vibe we find in Job:

> Then the LORD answered Job out of the whirlwind: . . .
> "Where were you when I laid the foundation of
>   the earth?
>   Tell me, if you have understanding.
> Who determined its measurements—surely you know!
>   Or who stretched the line upon it?
> On what were its bases sunk,
>   or who laid its cornerstone
> when the morning stars sang together
>   and all the heavenly beings shouted for joy?"
> (Job 38:1, 4-7)

As far as I'm concerned, it makes perfect sense that God would have used music to bring everything into existence, because creation is so full of music.

But there is also a way in which the wonder calls us into the future. The symphony of David's songs didn't reach their crescendo until much later, when they were embodied in

Jesus of Nazareth, "the anointed one." John 1:14 says "the Word became flesh and dwelt among us" (NKJV). We can rightly add that the music became flesh, because that is precisely what happened. Consider the mournful melody of Psalm 22:1, "My God, my God, why have you forsaken me?" and the tragic but triumphant music of Psalm 118:22: "The stone that the builders rejected has become the chief cornerstone." The music of Psalms was so embedded in Jesus of Nazareth that when He was tortured and killed, it wasn't just blood and gore that poured out of His ravaged body on the cross. As His body was squeezed and mangled, it was as if the music of the Psalms themselves oozed out. The music had so carried Him through life that it was the words of Psalm 31:5 that He exhaled with His final breaths: "Into your hand I commit my spirit."

I remember one of the first times I was captivated by wonder. It was during a middle school field trip to the planetarium. I ended up seated next to Crystal, a buxom girl with braces. Naturally, I was excited about this. But when the lights went down and the ceiling lit up with all the constellations, I was amazed enough by what I saw overhead to forget about her. As a city dweller who pretty much spent all my time at church in those days, I was mostly attuned to the kinds of signs and wonders one saw in the midst of a camp meeting. I was less into seeing nature and beauty or order in the cosmos as signs, and more into seeing crutches get broken and tossed aside. But the planetarium opened my eyes to a whole different realm.

I was arrested by wonder. Constellations are uniquely beautiful things, glorious patterns amid the galaxy's freckles.

I don't think it was an accident that the wise men, who were among the few to recognize Jesus for who He really was, were stargazers. In a sense, they were attuned to the music of the cosmos, and God used what was familiar to them to lead them to Himself. When they followed the stars far enough, they ultimately found themselves eyeball-to-eyeball with Jesus. I'm convinced that if we follow the wonder back to the source, if we follow the beauty all the way home, *we'll* find Jesus too.

How Jesus came to be *Jesus*

So many things are remarkable about Jesus from the moment He was born, that we can easily overlook the *process* He went through in pursuit of His calling. Even though He was born as the uniquely sinless Son of God, it still took a defining moment to set the course for everything He would do and become. Before He performed a single miracle, the perfect and anointed one needed a specific experience to prepare Him for all that was to follow. It was the moment, if you like, when Jesus became *Jesus*.

The story begins with a man named John, who like the wise men, had enough distance from the noise of culture to attend to the beauty of God. Because the legion was around long before the clutter of digital media, there have always been people who felt they had to move toward the margins of society to escape the noise. Not so they could escape "the real world" and bury their heads in the sand, but rather to escape *into* the real world, where they could actually see and hear.

Many scholars believe that John the Baptist was part of a fringe group called the Essenes, who lived out in the desert and practiced a strict form of Jewish religion. Like all people who live on the fringes of society, he was odd. His dress and diet were unconventional. There was something that felt a little wild about John. But because John withdrew himself from all the noise of the cities of his time, he heard the music.

As a man from the margins, John knew that he wasn't called to the main stage. His life's goal was to be an opening act. There was such a unique power and ferocity to John that many people believed he was the Messiah, the anointed one promised in the old texts. But John would have none of it. He said, "I baptize you with water; but one who is more powerful than I is coming; I am not worthy to untie the thong of his sandals" (Luke 3:16).

He sang the same song over and over again, calling people to repentance, until one day the main act—the headliner—showed up. Nobody had to tell John who Jesus really was. Somewhere deep in his soul, he just knew. He recognized the music.

God with skin on, the Word made flesh, the embodied song, showed up one day at the Jordan River, where John was pursuing his calling, baptizing people as a symbol of their repentance. In my mind's eye, I see John as his mouth went dry and his palms grew sticky, knowing this is the moment he'd been waiting for. John had a big voice, but I imagine these words coming out in a reverent whisper: "Behold, the Lamb of God, who takes away the sin of the world."[8]

John had been baptizing people in the wilderness. His sermons called people to stop taking advantage of each other and the poor, and baptism was a symbol that people were trading in their old ways of doing things. When Jesus appeared at the river, John knew there was no reason to call Him to repentance. Nonetheless, Jesus had come to be baptized. No longer the prophet with fire in his eyes, John was now the prophet with jelly in his legs. He was famous for not even being intimidated by kings, but now his coarse hands trembled.

When Jesus emerged from the water, the sky opened and the Spirit of God descended on Him like a dove.

And then came the voice.

"This is My beloved Son, in whom I am well pleased" (Matthew 3:17, NKJV).

These were the words of God Himself, and though only a handful, they were the most important words that Jesus would ever hear. These words were spoken before the oppressed and diseased were healed. They were spoken before He preached the Sermon on the Mount. They were spoken before He turned water into wine or walked on water.

They were words He would remember when His body was shutting down after forty days in the wilderness. They were words He'd remember when the crowds were shouting His name and singing to Him as if He were Caesar. They were words He'd remember when His best friends betrayed and abandoned Him. They were words He'd remember when His body was mangled and His beard was plucked out. The day would come when the face John touched so reverently would be so savaged that maybe even the music wouldn't have been enough for John to recognize Him. But the words would carry Him anyway, like a wave, from His bright-eyed beginning to His nightmarish death. The day would come when chunks of flesh would hang from His body, and His lungs would collapse. His body would be crushed, but the words would still remain: *You are my Son, the Beloved; with you I am well pleased.*[9]

The trajectory of Jesus' life and (in a real sense) the fate of the world hung on those few words. They were not the words of a Father celebrating the good things His Son had done, because He hadn't really done anything yet. Even though Jesus was perfect, it wasn't His perfection that brought the Father such delight. It was His very existence.

The language of God's passion litters the pages of the Old Testament—the word *beloved* is scattered through the stories of many human lives. But now, for the first time in human history, a man had come who really believed that He was the beloved of God, one who would always remember and would make every decision of His life based on the truth of those words.

Jesus was like us in many ways. Scripture says He was "in all points tempted as we are."[10] But of all the ways He was different from us, perhaps this is the most crucial one: *Jesus never forgot who He was.*

3
obscurity

✧ ✧ ✧

In solitude we realize that
nothing human is alien to us.
HENRI NOUWEN

In our culture, there's nothing worse than being obscure and
nothing better than being famous. For any reason or no reason whatsoever. We are endlessly infatuated with celebrities
and the thinly veiled fantasy that we might become celebrities ourselves. Like King Saul, the prospect of fame and adu-
lation seems to hold the keys to the universe for us. Never
mind that some of the most popular things in our culture are
mind-bendingly stupid, and many of our celebrity fixations
are with some of the least interesting people to have ever
walked the earth.

We export the debris of our popular culture all over the
planet. Last year, within a week of each other, I had ministry

trips to Kibera (Africa's second largest urban slum, near Nairobi, Kenya), and Beirut, Lebanon. I was stunned to see the impact of Western pop culture in such diverse places. In Kibera, while walking through the hardpan streets, with raw sewage running beneath my feet, I heard the sound of Jay-Z's "Empire State of Mind" coming from a little hut in which a family of ten lived in a single room. I walked into another hut where a teenager had stapled pictures of the pop/R & B singer Rihanna all over the wall. In all honesty, I think Jay-Z is a musical genius, but I could not even begin to comprehend what it means in our globalized economy to export his celebration of excess into a place like Kibera. It was equally striking to hear bands such as Nickelback on the radio in Beirut. If you haven't been riled up about injustice lately, consider this: Around the world right now, every three seconds, an impoverished child is exposed to Nickelback.

We know that the cultural assumptions undergirding our celebrity fetish are false, and not everything popular is good (and may, in fact, be profoundly bad), yet we continue to elevate and adulate people based on their ability to make a name for themselves. Then again, we live in a world that elected Saul and rejected Jesus. We are the kinds of people who would choose a good-looking leader ("he seems so presidential") but crucify the Son of Love. It is the nature of our mob instinct to pursue that which is superficial, shallow, and (in some cases) outright evil over that which is good. And we live our lives as if the extent to which we are broadly known, recognized, and celebrated somehow correlates to our value and worth.

It would be great if religious culture provided an oasis from our society's collective madness. Yet even in the church we sometimes trample each other in the race for fifteen minutes of fame or some small measure of worldly success. There is often little distinction between those the world and the church call "blessed." There is perhaps no one more likely to be surprised by those Jesus pronounces as blessed in the Sermon on the Mount than we are, conformed as we are to the world's system that praises that which is beautiful over that which is broken. To watch us, you'd have to conclude that by no means do we believe that those who are poor in spirit, those who mourn, those who are meek or merciful are by any means blessed. We don't believe that those who are persecuted or ridiculed are blessed. And certainly not the peacemakers. We have too many people to mock and ridicule, and peacemaking doesn't make for good television. Most of all, we hold out a faint hope that we, too, might one day be one of the beautiful people the world admires. Every child could be the next American Idol, or perhaps even president of the United States.

Why we need the wilderness

Saul, who is repeatedly depicted as "the people's choice" for king, was trapped in the endless cycle that characterizes ordinary people like us as much as it does kings: *Who is noticing me? Am I adequately appreciated and celebrated?* During the glory days of Saul's kingship, the brokenness and insecurity that made him desperately crave the adoration of the crowds was less conspicuous—he was so accustomed to it that he never really felt his own need. But all of that changed when the comparisons to David began.

There's a little of Saul in each of us. Comparing ourselves to other people is perhaps our most common universal pastime. If we look long enough and hard enough, we can always find someone who is more gifted than we are, who does the same things we do—only infinitely better—and thus we can feel bad about ourselves. Conversely, we identify people who are less gifted than we are, and against the backdrop of their lives we feel more confident and secure.

The only real antidote to the clamor of the crowd is time in the wilderness, where our true identity can be established and we can hear the still, small voice of God. Otherwise, it seems we have no way to determine our identity other than to compare ourselves with the people around us—who makes the most money, who drives the better car, who has more Facebook "friends," who is more or less successful than we are in our profession or parenting or upward mobility. As the world has become more accessible to us through the profusion of social media and the 24/7 news cycle, we have more exposure to more voices to approve or disapprove of us, and a wider "community" to notice or not notice us.

✧　✧　✧

As it was for Saul, inside each of us is a black hole of need, a vortex of insecurity. Because we live in a world that actively conspires against our being the boy on the bike or the girl on the trampoline, we find little time to just be ourselves. Few are the moments when we are truly at home in our own skin, happy with who we are and how we were created—moments when we can grasp God's delight. His voice of affirmation is not the least bit contingent on how we perform in any of our tasks, whether we are good at our jobs or even at spiritual practices. That's why it's so significant that God the Father spoke into His Son's identity *before* Jesus did any of the miracles or good works among the poor and marginalized. The Father's voice of love was the source from which the work of the Son would come— loving and accepting others as a natural extension of the love and blessing He had received. It could not work the other way around. He was the beloved Son *in* whom God was well pleased, not *by* whom He was well pleased. That distinction is critical.

The voice of the Father was rich in affirmation and acceptance, and the significance and mission of Jesus' life had never been clearer or more pronounced. Surely this was the right time to ride that momentum into productive ministry and service. No, the worst thing Jesus could have done after hearing the voice of His Father openly calling Him the Beloved would have been to immediately enter into the hustle and noise of society, or even into ministry. His mission was too important to risk that the voice of His Father might become just one among many other voices competing for His attention or affirming Him. Which is why it makes sense that the same Spirit of God that descended on Him also led Him into the wilderness.

The gift of the wilderness

In our culture of constant access and nonstop media, nothing feels more like a curse from God than time in the wilderness. To be obscure, to be off the beaten path, to be in the wilderness feels like abandonment. It seems more like exile than vacation. To be so far off of everyone's radar that the world might forget about us for a while? That's almost akin to death.

The notion of obscurity as a curse is so ingrained in our culture that even some people I know in vocational ministry feel that if they're not adequately known or recognized they've either done something wrong or God is unhappy with them. If only they knew that God draws people into obscurity—into the wilderness—not because He's angry with them or because they aren't "successful enough," but because He wants to go *deeper* in His relationship with them. Far from being punishment, judgment, or a curse, the wilderness is a *gift*. It's where we can experience the primal delight of being fully known and delighted in by God.

But we don't see it that way. From our parched perspective, the wilderness is a place of loneliness, doubt, and spiritual dryness—something to be avoided at all costs. Amid the constant noise of our daily lives, we don't have to reflect too deeply on what we're afraid of or what we're suppressing or even what we love. But the wilderness is where our demons come out to taunt us. That's why most of us don't want to go there.

And yet the reason that God sent Jesus into the wilderness was not to weaken Him—so that His showdown with Satan would become "the ultimate test"—but rather to strengthen Him and cement in His heart the truth of His identity. Fresh from hearing the words of confirmation on which His entire life and ministry would be built, there was no safer place than the wilderness for Jesus to go next. Even though His experience in the wilderness wasn't easy—He fasted for forty days and forty nights and was confronted by the devil—the devil was not the only one He encountered there. The Spirit sent Jesus into the wilderness, rejuvenated with the affirmation of His identity in God's eyes, and allowed Him to step away from His day-to-day life until the noise and hurry of the world around Him was stripped down to the point where He could easily distinguish the voice of the accuser from the voice of the Father. The same can be true for us.

For Satan, the wilderness is a place for attack. Away from the good gifts of friendship and community, it seems to be an opportunity to exploit our weaknesses and prey on our greatest fears. But more important, the wilderness is the place where God courts His beloved. When we step away from the noise and distraction, we find God has been wooing us all along.

When we feel far from God, the wilderness is the place where He draws us back to Himself. The writings of the prophet Hosea are teeming with the heartbreak of God reeling from rejection by His beloved. God takes the same risk that any of us take when we truly love someone—He loves in a way that gives the other person permission to hurt Him. Hosea 2 in particular contains the violent, catastrophic rage of a betrayed God. And yet even as it exposes a heart broken for His people, the darkness of the text unexpectedly gives way to unspeakable tenderness, to the characteristic beauty and delight of God for His wayward bride:

> Here's what I'm going to do:
>   I'm going to start all over again.
> I'm taking her back out into the wilderness
>   where we had our first date, and I'll court her.
>   (Hosea 2:14, MSG)

Jesus' entire life was in protest to the forces of evil, so it wasn't as if the wilderness was the only place where Satan was out to get Him. The devil doesn't talk to us more in the wilderness than elsewhere. But in the wilderness, away from all the noise, we're able to think clearly enough to identify him. In the wilderness, the devil's voice is more recognizable because it doesn't blend in with a legion of others.

Whether in the wilderness or in the midst of everyday life, the devil never has anything very original to say. In the wilderness narrative, he tempts Jesus three times:

If you are the Son of God, command these stones to become loaves of bread. (Matthew 4:3)

If you are the Son of God, throw yourself down [from the pinnacle of the Temple]; for it is written, . . . "You will not dash your foot against a stone." (Matthew 4:6)

All these [kingdoms] I will give you, if you will fall down and worship me. (Matthew 4:9)

The temptations are different, but the root is entirely the same: *If you are who you say you are . . . if you are who God says you are . . . then* prove *it to me. Prove it to the world.*

"*If* you are . . ."

When Satan comes after us with similar temptations, he plays on our deepest fears—that we won't be good enough, beautiful enough, smart enough, popular enough—that we won't be loved. *Fear's a powerful thing, baby. It can turn your heart black you can trust.*

But that's one way we can identify the devil's voice: It

always plays to our fears. It is the voice that tells us we must *do* something to prove who we are, to prove that we're worthy, to prove that we are who God has already declared us to be. When we know we are loved by God, we don't have to prove anything to anyone. There is nothing we can do to make ourselves more beloved than we are.

So when we hear the devil's catchphrase—"*If* you are . . ."—we can tune him out before he even finishes his sentence.

The tragedy for us, of course, is that we continually *forget* who we are. We catch a glimpse of our belovedness, but without the gift of the wilderness—those times of silence and solitude when we come face-to-face with ourselves and with God—it doesn't always stick. So as we re-immerse ourselves in the world of flashing screens, buzzing smartphones, and competing voices, we're prone to sliding back into doubt, discouragement, and disillusionment. We don't always hear the voice of the devil as it sounds in the wilderness—disjointed, absurd, obvious, easy to detect against the sparse landscape of solitude. Instead, we hear the devil's catchphrase everywhere, in and among all the other voices—from television to social media to the workplace to well-intentioned friends and family—shouting (or whispering), "If you are _____, then prove it."

In a world of nonstop connectivity, the question is less, Where do we hear the devil? and more, When do we *not* hear the devil? That's not to say that every voice in the

world is satanic—let's not give more credit than is due—
but our enemy is wily, and he leverages whatever he can to
his advantage, even if all he can do is pump up the volume
to try to drown out the voice of God.

Most of us have at least a handful of people in our lives
who truly love us for who we are and not for what we can
do. The rest of the world cares for us only to the extent that
we meet their expectations. Most of the voices we hear
come from people who want something from us. No wonder it's so hard to tune our hearts to the voice of the one
who calls us beloved just because we're His.

Finding the wilderness in the twenty-first century

Everyone needs time in the wilderness. Everyone needs
time to be alone—and silent. But with our constant connectivity, we're rarely alone when we are alone and rarely
together when we are together.

I love the title of Sherry Turkle's brilliant book *Alone
Together: Why We Expect More from Technology and Less from
Each Other*. Turkle, a clinical psychologist and professor at
MIT, has spent her career studying the ways in which our
technology changes us. Her earlier work was optimistic
about how our relationship to machines affects human
thought, memory, and understanding.

Alone Together is more a cautionary tale, though not
intended to scare us off of our technology altogether. But
as the world has changed, Turkle has seen the need for us

to reflect seriously on the danger of allowing technology to dictate to us. This, incidentally, is one of the clearest hall-marks of the devil's work—the voice of the accuser is always compulsory and aggressive (whereas the voice that calls us beloved always leads us gently). We feel driven to interact online constantly and yet without true intimacy. Turkle describes an event she attended in a large confer-ence hall in Tokyo, where everyone was busy on their laptops, and the feeling she had that this mass of people sharing the same space were all in different worlds.

Paradoxically, it is our very need for intimacy that draws us to technology, and yet the illusion of closeness that comes from constant contact goes hand-in-hand with the relative safety and emotional distance of indirect communi-cation. We feel that we can be more honest online when we don't have to look the other person in the eye or even use our real identity. Turkle observes, "These days, insecure in our relationships and anxious about intimacy, we look to technology for ways to be in relationships and protect our-selves from them at the same time."[1] In this new world, we "fear the risks and disappointments of relationships with our fellow humans."[2] Hence, people report spending many hours online interacting with other people and yet feel pro-foundly alone and detached. We now have constant access to a legion of voices with differing expectations, and yet we never feel fully known.

I don't think this technology is intrinsically bad or "demonic," but I do think we need to recognize how

technology defines the character of many of our relationships, and ask ourselves why we feel the need to become
something other than who we are or to "do something" to
prove our worth.

✧　✧　✧

In its capacity to strip away false intimacy and call us back
to a place of being fully known and completely loved, the
gift of the wilderness is beautiful and yet profoundly difficult. The "withdrawal symptoms" attendant on our pulling
away for a few moments from constant connectivity can be
unnerving. Sherry Turkle talks about the "phantom limb"
of the cell phone—how teenagers report being able to hear
their cell phones ring even while stashed away in their lock-
ers as required by school rules.[3] The continual stimulation
of the "you've got mail" feature of our e-mail in-boxes, as
much as we might claim to hate it, is nonetheless validat-
ing. It says we are needed, we are important, we are
valuable.

A couple of years ago, I decided to become more inten-
tional about going into the wilderness on a regular basis. It
was the Spirit who led me there, and as in Hosea, the purpose was always to speak tenderly to me there, to court me.
But as it was for Jesus, the transition to the wilderness was
jarring at first.

On my first foray, I went to spend a week at the Abbey
of Gethsemani in New Haven, Kentucky, known to the
world as the Trappist monastery where Thomas Merton

spent his monastic career. The Trappist order is silent most of the time, performing their duties and eating their meals in silence. Because I've known the strain, at times, of always feeling pulled on and needed, and because I am beholden to a legion of voices that tell me I must prove something of my identity to the world, I couldn't wait to get to the abbey. I remember driving through the mountains of West Virginia and on into Kentucky with the windows down and rock music blaring, intoxicated by the idea of wilderness time.

The problem, of course, was that the reality of wilderness time was far different from the idea of it. Having grown up Pentecostal, I've never been comfortable with silence. And being a know-it-all big-mouth in the ways that preachers are inclined to be, and suffering from the unique psychosis of thinking I have something worth saying about life for an hour every week that the world needs to hear, silence is not native to my personality. Still, armed with my Bible, my journal, and a handful of spiritual books, I felt I was ready for the exotic wilderness.

You can imagine my surprise when, for the first couple of days, I mostly felt as if my soul was throwing up. I might complain about my attachment to my cell phone and the demands of all the people back home who say they need me, but who am I without them? My identity was wrapped up in the legion of voices assigned to me, each with its own set of expectations and its own opinions about who I am and who I'm called to be. Even if at times I feel overwhelmed by them—"It feels like a thousand voices are competing for my attention!"—surely there is a part of me that finds the voices of the legion seductive. Instead of being repelled by all the clamor, I rather enjoy being the center of my own universe. So I hear it as, "A thousand voices are competing for my attention. I must be *really* important."

It's not as if all the voices we hear are demonic, that everyone who expects something of us or attempts to define us in the way that humans do is somehow the tool of Satan. It is rather that the evil one, the maestro of malice, conducts these voices into a symphony of constant distraction that keeps us from grabbing hold of who we really are and what we are called to become.

It is painful at first to realize that the complex web of online and off-line relationships we use are actually using us. That though we get brief and fleeting glimpses of identity through them, we lack the fulfillment that comes to us only through the one who says we are beloved for no other reason than that we exist. It is jarring to realize that no other identity besides son or daughter of the King gives our lives ultimate meaning and significance.

I have learned that breaking out from the legion of voices in my life to enter the rhythm of monastic life is very good for my soul. The Trappist monks orient their days around the seven daily offices or prayers, starting at 3:15 each morning. I love to go and chant the Psalms with them, even though the liturgy is foreign to me. The Psalms teach us many things, but it seems we never go more than a verse or two without running smack-dab into our beloved-ness again. In those daily prayer times at the monastery, I am reminded of who I really am.

I have also been reminded that my need to prove my identity, even to God, is insidious and easily concealed. And the voices that say, "If you are who God says you are, prove it," can follow me even into spiritual retreat.

When I embarked on my latest "wilderness trip"—this time down to the beautiful Mepkin Abbey in Moncks Corner, South Carolina, which is also a Trappist order—true to form, I was ready to approach the scheduled prayer times with my resident legalistic fervor. And I felt really bad about missing any of them. I had a certain, teeth-gritting determination to hear God in the wilderness by doing all the right things. So I was surprised one morning when I was overcome by the sense that I needed to go to the beach. Mepkin Abbey is about an hour and fifteen minutes from Seabrook Island, the site of my flagship boy-on-the-bike encounter. Despite my determination to stay focused on my "program," I could not shake the sensation that I had to get to the beach, and soon.

After wrestling with the feeling for a while, I blew off the prayer times, got in my car, and drove to Seabrook. Along the way, I rented a bike to take with me. When I reached the island, armed with a cooler and my journal, I rode the bike to the beach. By the time I actually sat down on the sand, my mind was so flooded with the goodness and beauty of God that I felt as if my head would explode. The music I heard was so sweet and profound, the clarity of life and min- istry that broke through all the complexities was so pro- nounced, that I couldn't write fast enough in my journal. The presence that had eluded me at the monastery was strong on the beach, where I sat in my swim trunks, slath- ered in suntan lotion, with tears staining the pages of my journal while I wrote as if under a spell.

In my attempt to go into the wilderness on my "spiri- tual retreat," I had not yet gone deep enough. I thought the object of the time was to immerse myself in prayer and Scripture. I forgot that the object was actually God, and that real prayer is what happens when my head and heart are fully exposed to Him.

God hadn't drawn me into the wilderness so I could attempt to prove myself to Him with religious activity (instead of the more secular activities I indulge in to prove myself to everyone else). He hadn't brought me away from the hustle and noise so I could demonstrate my spirituality to Him. He brought me out to allure me. He didn't want my performance, He wanted my attention. And at that point I don't believe He was drawing me to a place where I could talk to Him. He was drawing me to a place where He could talk to me.

The fruit of obscurity

Obscurity is not punishment. The wilderness is the place where our identity is solidified. The wilderness has its perils, to be sure; yet in a sense, there is no safer place. In the wilderness we find out who we really are. We find out what we're afraid of. We find out who our enemies are.

Though the obscurity of the wilderness brings divine allurement, that doesn't mean it's an easy place to be. I had a long list of things that I felt I needed to accomplish before I turned thirty, in order to feel successful in ministry. I didn't get much of it done. Instead, there were long seasons of silent disappointment. When I was first starting out, there were times when I felt upwardly mobile. Like many people both in the church and in the world at large, I assumed that what was best for me was to always be climbing higher and getting more—more influence, more people, a bigger platform. But just when it seemed I was starting to get some traction, I would feel God nudging me into the wilderness. This happened repeatedly. I felt I was ready to graduate into the Promised Land. I was sure of it. All the while, I was looking over my shoulder at other people, comparing my progress to theirs and thinking that, with my gifts, I should be where they are or perhaps even further along.

One thing for certain, the wilderness will reveal the brokenness and imperfections that lurk within us. I resented the feeling that God was constantly telling me to work on the foundation, because foundation building is very unsexy, underground work.

The beautiful thing about all of this, which I'm finally able to see, is that in the wilderness I both encountered

God and came to fully understand the depth of my own brokenness.

When I say things like that as a pastor, I think people sometimes think I'm just trying to relate or acting like I'm one of the boys. But I'm not just putting on the cloak of humility here. Over and over again, the wilderness has revealed the extent to which I am a wreck and the subversive ego that lies just beneath my humble-bumble preacher platitudes.

When we come face-to-face with our own demons and stare them down in the wilderness, it will put some years on our souls. Because I grew up in a parsonage, I always felt like I was aged in dog years by the church anyway. But I've got the leathered skin in my soul and the entrenched wrinkles of a construction worker from all the wilderness living I've done.

One of the greatest gifts of the wilderness is that it has rendered me much less likely to ever be impressed with myself. I'm too well acquainted with myself by now to believe my own PR. If people are overly impressed with me, they simply don't know me well enough yet.

On the other hand, the wilderness also reveals the staggering depth of God's love for us, every bit as much as it spotlights the devils we let camp out on our shoulders. It is a remarkable thing to simultaneously have our brokenness and belovedness revealed in equal measure.

I am now grateful for the kindness of God in allowing me to have so many of the same opportunities I once craved so desperately. Only now my focus is on Him, rather than on all I hope to achieve (or prove). The wilderness gives us the insulation we need to handle success and failure equally well.

There was a time in my life when the book you hold in your hands would not have been just paper and ink (or an e-reader download). Instead, it would have been the ruler by which I measured God's love for me and my value to the world. Thank God, the stakes aren't nearly so high with such things these days. Criticism can still sting me, but it cannot shatter the revelation of my identity as a beloved son of God. On the other hand, I can't get quite as excited as I once did by people's affirmation of me. I love to be encouraged and appreciated as much as anybody, but I know that nothing kind you might say about me would change the reality of what I've seen in myself in the wilderness. I am both more loved and more broken than you could possibly know.

One of the key differences between David and Saul is that Saul, the people's champion, got drunk on human affirmation at an early age. David, on the other hand, was intoxicated by the beauty of God's creation and punch drunk on the knowledge of God's love for him.

You may think you're in obscurity right now because you've done something wrong. You may think you're in the wilderness because you've been cursed or abandoned by God. But if you're in the wilderness, I'd like to suggest it's because you are so desperately loved. What if you're living in obscurity because God is so intent on showing you things about yourself that you would not otherwise see and revealing things about His love that you would not otherwise know?

Obscurity is where God sends all of His favorite sons and daughters. Our society tells us that if and when we get "there"—the job or position or degree we've always wanted, the notoriety we've always dreamed of—that's when all the important stuff will start happening. Not so.

All the good stuff happens in obscurity.

4
calling

✧ ✧ ✧

The place God calls you to is the place where your deep
gladness and the world's deep hunger meet.
FREDERICK BUECHNER

Here's the beautiful thing about obscurity: It leads to *call-ing*. Throughout our lives, we will be sent into the wilderness to remember or rediscover who God is and who He says we are, but it is also from deep within our wilderness obscurity that we are called out into the world. Whether or not popular culture ever knows or celebrates our name, God will give us futuristic work to do. We are called to bring the future acceptance of God's good and imminent reign back into the world, which still operates on antiquated definitions of success and worth.

The fact that broken people like us seem far too unstable and undependable to bring the futuristic contours of God's Kingdom of love into the world may be precisely what makes us the most likely candidates. It's just how God does things—like choosing a murderer with a speech impediment (Moses) or an obscure shepherd boy who would commit both adultery and murder (David) to lead His people. It is always the most unlikely people who do the most astonishingly beautiful good work in God's Kingdom. The fact that your current station in life would seem to conspire against your usefulness to God is of no consequence.

Even after you begin to receive the revelation of your belovedness, it's quite common for nothing much to change in your life. When he was still just a boy, David was anointed by Samuel to become king, but the road to fulfillment involved many years of literal wilderness wandering. In fact, before David was elevated to the kingship of Israel, he seemed to bottom out completely—feigning madness with a loogie hanging from his beard while trying to keep a Philistine king from killing him. He hardly looks as if he's en route to a throne.

When the time came for the future king to build an army, they looked even less impressive than he did: "Everyone who was in distress, and everyone who was in debt, and everyone who was discontented gathered to him; and he became captain over them" (1 Samuel 22:2). These were hardly Navy SEALs.

If you are going to build a great army, do you honestly think that malcontents and debtors make the best candidates? These people didn't have noble motives. They weren't looking to do something great in the world. They weren't even looking to do something great for David. They were unemployed and down and out. What else were they going to do? They were people from the margins who gathered around David for no other reason than that he, too, was on the margins, on the run from King Saul.

Jesus used the same award-winning business principle when He put together His band of disciples. Do any of those rather obstinate fishermen seem qualified to help inaugurate a global movement? In Acts, we're told that the main reason people believed that God was at work in the lives of Peter and John was because the disciples proclaimed the truth about Jesus with *boldness*, despite the fact that they were "uneducated and ordinary men" (Acts 4:13).

I wish Jesus had read Jim Collins's *Good to Great* so He could have gotten the right people on the bus and then the right people in the right seats on the bus. At the very least, He should have run the Myers-Briggs profile on them to ensure that everyone had the right gift mix and He wasn't accidentally putting an ESTJ together with an INFP and causing a personality conflict.

Yet it seems as if everywhere Jesus went, the same people showed up: those who had nowhere else to go and nothing better to do. In the Gospels, Jesus is called the light of the world. Apparently, whores and thieves and the sick and demon-possessed are the moths He attracts.

Liars, dreamers, and misfits

It seems like a recipe for disaster: "Everyone who was in distress, and everyone who was in debt, and everyone who was discontented . . ." I love that verse because for me it describes the first church plant in history. When we started Renovatus in 2006, I learned firsthand that when you start something small on the margins, all the crazies come out. Everyone who doesn't fit in somewhere else comes to you. Everyone who has tried eight different churches in town and has been oddly misunderstood in each of them. Everyone who feels they've been overlooked. Might I add that many times there are good reasons why they haven't been able to get along well with anyone, and valid reasons why they didn't fit in!

We adapted language from Shel Silverstein's poem "Invitation" to say that we are a church "for liars, dreamers, and misfits." From David's comically titled "mighty men" to Jesus' random band of fishermen-and-tax-collectors-turned-disciples, nobody God picks to change the world seems suited for the job. So we decided to embrace this reality. It's why we call Renovatus "a church for people under renovation." We wanted to start from the premise that we are all basically train wrecks, in one way or another, and thus we all need an ongoing process of transformation and renewal.

The renovation motif ran throughout the places we went and the people we picked up. A couple of years in, we moved into the old movie theater in our city's most disreputable mall. It was the first time we got ourselves on the map of our city. Everyone from the *Charlotte Observer* to the alternative independent *Creative Loafing* covered the story. The general sentiment went something like this: "It's great that a church would want to meet at Eastland Mall. *I* would never go to a church there, but it's great that a church would want to be there." All the anchor stores had moved out of Eastland because of all the violence and poverty—not only in the neighborhood but inside the mall itself. A guy was shot and killed in the food court. Several people had been stabbed. There were gang problems. The theater still looked its 1975 age, a place where people came to watch *Jaws* and *The Rocky Horror Picture Show.*

By relocating where we did, we opened up our congregation to a whole new group of people, including Casim, now one of the key volunteers in our college and young adult ministry. Casim spent most of his formative years being ridiculed by significant men in his life. Nobody ever spoke to his belovedness as a son of God. From an early age, he learned to get attention by turning tricks for money. One evening, just after a rendezvous with a client in a public bathroom in the mall, Casim walked past the theater on his way out to his car, and some college students hanging out in the lobby offered him something to eat. A few minutes later, he was listening to Pastor Teddy Hart preach about Jesus. Two weeks later, he came crashing head-on into his belovedness. And he's never been the same.

Pastor Teddy went to Lee University, a Christian college in Cleveland, Tennessee. He managed to live there for seven years without completing his undergraduate degree. I know a lot of people who went to school with Teddy, because Lee University is part of my native denomination and, well, Teddy was there for a long time. They all tell me what a delight he was. Like the day he was playing basketball and talked trash to a youth pastor in anatomical language I cannot repeat unless you buy the unrated director's cut of my book. The youth pastor punched Teddy in the mouth and knocked his teeth out.

To be clear, Teddy has teeth today, which is probably the closest thing to a credential he has for being a college and young adult pastor. I mean, besides the fact that he told me the first day I met him at the Zaxby's in Cleveland that he felt there was a calling on his life for something more than screen-printing T-shirts. Teddy had initially forgotten about our lunch appointment, as he had been up until 6:00 a.m. from the night before in a high-stakes poker game in Chattanooga. I liked him immediately, and I was in no position really to demand much in the way of résumés. So I made him an offer he could not refuse: Why don't you move down to Charlotte and come to work at our new church plant, without a paycheck? Misfits and dreamers are far more likely to accept an offer like that.

Though the theater was close to full the night Casim wandered in, on Teddy's first night conducting the young adult group we call Dust, we gifted him with four of the

coolest homeschooled nineteen-year-olds you've ever met.
I think they were all dropped off by their mothers. It had
all the makings of a trendy college ministry, for sure. Today
Teddy leads the most thriving young adult ministry I've
seen, and he's a guy I'm happy to have preach to our entire
congregation on any given Sunday.

Blake Blackman is the guest services director at our
church. When I met her, she was still trying to drink and
party away her grief at the loss of a one-year-old son a few
years earlier. She worked behind the counter at the
Common Market Deli in my neighborhood. The day she
found out I was a pastor, she was wearing a T-shirt with a
picture of Jesus wearing a crown of thorns and an eye
patch, with the caption "God is my co-pirate." Now she's
responsible for the army of volunteers who produce our
worship services in both Charlotte, North Carolina, and
Fort Mill, South Carolina.

I could go on and on. Our brilliant worship arts pastor,
Sarah DeShields, managed a part-time job at Starbucks
when I met her. She was from Scotland and had shining
credentials but had trouble getting a green card. She married a guitarist in our church and released her first solo
worship album in 2012. And then there are the key leaders
in our church who got run out of the churches they last
attended due to personality conflicts and moral failures.

As we moved into different locations, the renovation
theme kept gaining traction. We hold Sunday services in
a building that once housed Jim and Tammy Bakker's

television show during the PTL years. Our facility in West Charlotte was originally home to a church best known for protesting everything and everybody. The former pastor, a far–right wing political activist, did many things that became infamous in our city, such as protesting the nudity and homosexual themes of the play *Angels in America* when it ran in Charlotte. This, of course, makes this stigmatized property a wonderful place for a Renovatus congregation that started off focusing on ministry to folks in our city affected by HIV/AIDS.

Misfit lifeguards

It might seem strange that people who have spent much of their lives on the margins, products of the wilderness by choice or by compulsion—but either way, by the Spirit— would end up doing such good in the world by serving others. But it's the way God does things. Spending time in obscurity in general, and in the wilderness in particular, allows us not only to be loved in our brokenness, but also to have the heartbreak of God for the broken people around us tattooed on our hearts. Aware of our own deep inadequacies but learning to accept that we are loved by God, we begin to share in His promiscuous love for the broken people around us.

Visiting my favorite comic-book shop one day, I heard a large, awkward guy, who was ahead of me in line, pontificating about the universe of the Transformers as if it were the Israeli-Palestinian peace process. Everything about his manner and appearance said he lived at home when he really should probably have a condo and a day job by now, that he eats too many donuts and plays too many video games and feels more alive on the Second Life website or an online gaming forum than he does at a party. I was immediately drawn to him, and I wished we could be brothers, telling inappropriate jokes and talking about Marvel Comics deep into the night.

Another day, at a restaurant, the young waitress let down her guarded politeness and artificial banter for a moment and a bit of her story leaked out from just behind the eyes. All of a sudden, I saw a glimpse of her as a daughter, a sister, and the girlfriend of some guy in community college, and I wished we could sit down for a few hours so she could tell me about her pain and her victories and I could tell her about Jesus. That wasn't a special day. It was just a Wednesday.

None of this comes from a pious disposition or a condescending desire to swoop in and "save" anyone. I still need saving myself too desperately for that. When we started our church, I fancied myself the charismatic, stable front man for our band of liars, dreamers, and misfits—after all, you need someone who is together to show everyone else what they might become, right? What a farce! Most days, I'm more like David, the broken runaway fleeing from King Saul, feigning madness, with the loogie running from my beard, doing the best I can to survive. If there is anything in me that draws broken people into wholeness, it is the one who hovers over me and whispers "beloved" into my ear, even while my sweaty hair is matted to my madman's brow.

Even as I have learned to live more deeply into my identity as God's beloved, I do not see perfectly. Like the blind man Jesus touched who then said he saw men as trees,[1] I keep having to go back for another touch in order to see what He sees. But when He touches my eyes, what I can see! I see the world the way He saw me: not just a broken man, but a king in development; not just for my past but for my potential. You can spot people who don't know Jesus very well because the world they see is always so ugly. Even if they use all sorts of religious language, don't be misled—people who get touched by Jesus don't ignore the hurt and pain in the world, and yet they see so much beauty in it. They see beauty because they see the future breaking into the present. They see both the beauty in the broken people around them and the beauty that is yet to come when they know their identity as the beloved. I think often of Thomas Merton's epiphany standing on a street corner:

In Louisville, at the corner of Fourth and Walnut, in the center of the shopping district, I was suddenly overwhelmed with the realization that I loved all those people, that they were mine and I theirs, that we could not be alien to one another even though we were total strangers. . . .

I have the immense joy of being *man*, a member
of the race in which God Himself became incarnate.
As if the sorrows and stupidities of the human
condition could overwhelm me, now I realize what
we all are. And if only everybody could realize this!
But it cannot be explained. There is no way of telling
people that they are all walking around shining like
the sun.[2]

The woman

Everywhere Jesus went, people who had been pushed to the
margins began to see themselves in a new light. And as they
came to know how beloved they were, they began to act in
ways that defied tradition and cultural expectations. These
stories are emotional land mines of dignifying love that
litter the field of the Gospel narratives, and there are too
many for me to recount here. But one story is my favorite.

The scene is the dining room of a prominent religious
leader. Between the animated conversation, punctuated with
moments of uproarious laughter and the clink of goblets, it
was easy for a young woman to slink into the back of the
room. There was far too much commotion for her to be
noticed. Besides, all eyes were focused on Jesus of Nazareth,
the controversial prophet whose teachings were beginning to
catch fire in the village. Rumors were flying that He was
some sort of miracle worker. Some were so impressed by His
teaching that they were already whispering that He was the

second coming of Elijah. Others were calling Him a charla-
tan. Still others couldn't deny the veracity of the miracles but
said the audacity of His teaching showed Him to be a blas-
phemer. While opinions were diverse, what was certain was
that He had captured the imagination of the village. Critics
and sympathizers alike had shown up from all over town to
get a glimpse of the itinerant prophet firsthand, and so far
the evening had not disappointed.

Though we have no reason to believe Jesus was physically imposing, His gentle charisma and generosity of spirit
seemed too big for the room. Even those most suspicious of
this upstart, would-be prophet were spellbound by the stories He told. His demeanor was humble and gracious, but
He wasn't afraid to laugh at His own jokes. Of course,
some said He had an ego that was out of control and that
He was aggrandizing Himself by identifying with the
prophets of old; but even His harshest critics couldn't deny
there was something genuinely magnetic about the man at
the end of the table. It didn't feel as if He were putting on
airs or trying to think of the right thing to say—He
answered their questions so casually, almost thoughtlessly,
that it was honestly a bit unnerving. He was utterly devoid
of pretense, and long after the night was over, they would
say they had never seen anyone so comfortable in his own
skin. It wasn't just *what* He said—it was the way He said it.
Whenever anyone asked a question, He looked at them
with such genuine tenderness it was almost heartbreaking.
Whether He was the next underground revolutionary to

rev up angry Jews against their Roman oppressors, a heretic teacher, or a glorified magician, the night belonged to Him. The wealthy guests and highbrow clerics were all spell-bound. The love that radiated from the young prophet was almost hypnotic, and they stared at Him as if they were in a trance.

This was all good for the woman, who was making every effort not to draw attention to herself. Half the men in the room had called her a whore and the other half had used her as one, so she was hardly at home in the social scene.[3] Yet, even for the handful who noticed her creep in like a house cat, there was no reason for alarm. On a less auspicious night, her presence might provoke a few whispers and a few more stares. But this was the kind of night when everybody who was anybody and everybody who was nobody all showed up, such was the spectacle of the enigmatic dinner guest. In the circus-like atmosphere created by the village grapevine, not even a reputed prostitute could be blamed for coming to see what the hoopla was all about.

For a few moments, she stood against the back wall, so entranced by the symphony of the man's words that she almost forgot where she was and why she had come. There was such loveliness in His voice as it poured over her. She had no desire to make a scene—for a moment at least, just to be within a few feet of Him was enough for her. But when the smoky aroma of the lamb wafted away from her, she caught a faint whiff of the perfume in her tiny box and fell out of orbit.

Ever since her first fateful encounter with Jesus a few months prior, she had saved every penny to find a way to thank Him for what He had done for her. In only a few short moments with Him, there had been a transaction within her that couldn't be undone. She had become immune to the low-grade hum of whispers and the chorus of eyes that followed her around like wolves everywhere she walked.

Although it was her business to traffic in nakedness, she had never felt quite as exposed as she had the day she met Jesus of Nazareth—fully clothed. For all the eyes that had leered at her when she walked through town, in meeting Him it was as if it were the first time anybody had actually seen her. Though she'd been groped by the calloused hands of hundreds of "lovers," she had never felt such a human touch as she did that day. There was nothing erotic about it. His gaze was so exquisitely tender, so free of want and lust and expectation that it nearly devastated her. He looked at her as if He'd known her face before the world was made. He saw her as a newborn daughter, a stunning bride, and the respectable grandmother she knew she'd never become. His look seemed to sum up all the days of her past and all the days yet to come, a look that knew where she'd been and where she had yet to go. He saw her completely as a woman, but even more so, He saw her as a precious human being. Her suggestive good looks had elicited the false intimacy of loving words spoken by countless men in the darkness. But this was the first time anyone had made her feel completely loved.

Ever since that first encounter, she'd saved to buy a vial of nard, the most expensive oil in the market. She knew that the love she felt that day was so extravagant that a river of perfume wouldn't do justice to the man who had brought her to life, but it was, nonetheless, the most extravagant gesture she could afford. Today she carried her box of perfume as delicately as if carrying a dozen quail eggs, careful to make sure she didn't drop it.

Then suddenly she knew that it was her moment. Though what she had planned was likely to get the old wives' tongues wagging and the old clerics' brows furrowed, she couldn't think about that now. The last thing she wanted was to tarnish His reputation, for people to suspect that the charismatic prophet was her client. But the sheer velocity of love and gratitude burning through her veins was more powerful than any of her other concerns. And though she felt her stomach turn to hot liquid and her mouth go dry, she lunged forward like a madwoman from the back wall and ran to the head of the table. By the time she reached Him, she was weeping. Grabbing His feet, His beautiful, beautiful feet, she let the lava of her tears fall onto His toes. She hung on like a newborn baby, holding and caressing His feet, showering them with salt water. For a moment, she could feel the eyes of the crowd boring into the back of her head, but she didn't care. Although her eyes were too misty to see anything, she could feel the tenderness of His gaze, and that was all that mattered.

Acting out of an adoration as instinctive as breathing, she began to kiss His feet—not once or twice, but over and over again, almost manically. The agents of social convention arrayed about the table looked at her with dignified disgust, as if she had undressed herself. But if the truth of that moment were ever truly told (and among the religious and social elite with ringside seats the truth was more than they could afford to tell), what surprised them was not how erotic her kisses were, but how pure. Her lips grazed His dusty feet so reverently, it was almost unbearable to watch. The innocence and joy of her worship was so genuine that it felt like an indictment against the good manners and hollow religious posturing of all the guests of honor.

The enchanting spell of the young storyteller was now fully broken as all eyes glared at the spectacle before them, her body a crumpled heap on the floor. Wasting no time, she took the bottle of nard—a year's worth of wages—and drenched Jesus' feet with it. When the bottle burst, it did not trickle. It gushed. There was nothing slow and methodical or ceremonious about her act. It was hasty and decisive. Before the smell of the expensive perfume filled the house, the liquid was already gone in a shocking act of waste.

The little money she had left after purchasing the perfume she had used to have her hair washed, and if you had gotten close enough you might have smelled the flowery fragrance mingling with the profusion of exotic perfume. With her hair clean and curled and pretty, and her nose and lips still pressed against the soft skin on the topside of Jesus' feet, she draped her hair across His toes and began to dry them. Using her hands to wrap her tresses tightly around His feet, she used her beautiful hair, her glory, as if it were a cheap rag for washing dishes, mindful only of letting Him know how deeply she loved Him.

It was a scene too lovely for angels, and yet the other guests glared at her as if they had seen something vulgar instead of something unspeakably holy. Jesus was the only one left unrattled, His demeanor as easy and at home as it had been before the woman's volcano of tears erupted. With His otherworldly ability to read people's motives and emotions, surely He sensed the contempt that settled over the room like a dense fog. Yet when He directed His gaze at Simon, the host of the dinner, His eyes were no less tender than when He had looked at the woman at His feet. As if there had not been a catastrophic breach of social etiquette in the middle of the room, He addressed His host in the same easy manner as before.

"I need to ask you something, Simon."

"What is it, Rabbi?"

"Two people owed the same moneylender. One owed him five hundred dollars, the other owed him fifty. Neither one had enough to pay him back, so he decided to forgive both of their debts. Now, which of the two do you suppose will love him more?"

Simon's eyes shifted to the floor. "I suppose the one who had the bigger debt."

"You got it," Jesus said, His eyes sparkling.

Then He turned to the woman, whose hair still grazed the top of His feet, and said to Simon, "Do you see this woman? When I came into your house, you did not give me any water for my feet, but she wet my feet with her tears and wiped them with her hair. You did not give me a kiss, but she has not stopped kissing my feet since she got here. You did not pour oil over my head, but she has poured perfume on my feet. Therefore, I tell you, her many sins have been forgiven—as her great love has shown. But whoever has been forgiven little loves little."

Then Jesus said to the woman, "Your sins are forgiven."

The air of polite contempt turned quickly bitter as the whispers started: "Who is He that He even forgives sins?"

Jesus said to the woman, "Your faith has saved you; go in peace."

I understand that stories like mine and Casim's and Blake's and Teddy's and that of the anonymous woman at the feet of Jesus may seem odd to you. It's true that we're a motley bunch. We aren't exactly the sort of people who would gravitate to one another in a singles bar. All we have in common is a deep-seated brokenness and a deep need for the one who called us beloved.

Like the woman in the story, we are doing strange things by the customs of the world. Our newfound identity as beloved of God makes us act in ways that, frankly, scare the natives. Most of all, we're shaking up the religious folks. But like the woman in the story, we don't have much time to worry about what the townspeople are saying. The way that Jesus has accepted us makes us lovesick for Him, and in turn He's beginning to make us lovesick for others.

We are not an exclusive lot. There is room in the band of liars, dreamers, and misfits if you want to audition. The only qualification necessary for membership is that you fail the audition, in which case I'm quite confident you've got what it takes.

5
wounds

✧ ✧ ✧

I can with one eye squinted take it all as a blessing.
FLANNERY O'CONNOR

If there is a moment when everyone was the boy on a bike or the girl on a trampoline, if there was a time of innocence and naiveté when we were tantalized with a world beyond our own, there was also a moment when that world came crashing down. When I was the boy on the bike, I knew nothing about suffering or pain. Cruising the neighborhood on my time machine, back and forth between trips to outer space, I felt indestructible. I had yet to lose anyone significant in my life. Most of all, I was blissfully unaware of just how easily my fragile eight-year-old body could break.

Wouldn't you like to recapture something of the wonder

that came as natural as breathing in those days? The idea of a second naiveté has some merit. But many things have changed since then. It isn't just that we've gotten older and wiser. We've also collected scars. We've accumulated wounds.

Our scars are more than just the sum total of our tragic memories. Scars speak of identity, of calling. Scars speak the truth of who we are beneath the deception of our façades. It's no wonder that when Paul wrote to the early Christian communities, he always spoke of the scars he had accumulated from persecution for the sake of Jesus' name.[1] The message embedded in our scars, the code encrypted implicitly beneath ruptured skin or emotions, is not just about our pain, but about God's faithfulness. Scars tell the story of who we really are and where we've really come from, even when we refuse to speak the truth with our eyes or our lips (or even to ourselves). Like the rings on the interior of a tree, everything you could ever want to know about people can be read from their scars.

It's not exactly an icebreaker for a party, but if we really wanted to get to know each other, we would ask to see each other's scars. It's a dangerous and impolite question to ask, and not necessarily the level of community we even consciously desire, but when nothing else in our lives (including our words) rings true, we can always rely on our scars to tell the truth.

We all want to avoid suffering at all costs. We assume that whatever has wounded us, whatever has scarred us, is now an obstacle to all that we are supposed to become.

And yet that's the beauty, or genius, of Jesus' whole new way of being human—in Him, our scars are no longer a source of shame. In fact (and this is perhaps the most revolutionary part), our scars, in a sense, *authenticate* us. After Christ's resurrection, the disciples were able to recognize Him by His scars. The wounds inflicted on Him on the cross told a story that the world needed to hear.

This is part of what it means to follow Jesus in becoming people from the future: We become the kind of people who no longer have to hide their scars. Our scars reveal who we are. The fact that we have experienced profound suffering in life—the fact that we carry what may seem to be unsightly scars—does not disqualify us from following Jesus. It may be precisely what qualifies us.

Bullied

The story of my first scar is not especially tragic by most standards. But like many of our wounds, it came at the hands of a bully. I was in second grade and living in Kannapolis. I was already frightened out of my mind about Nostradamus, the Antichrist, and the end of the world, and then I had the misfortune to encounter Gus, a boy from the neighborhood who was three years older and a whole lot bigger than I was.

Despite my fears, I was still very much, at that point in my life, the boy on the bike—a child of wonder, familiar with God, and thus familiar with love and awe of the world. Riding my bike was where I felt the most safe and alive. That is, until the day Gus came over on his own bike after school.

I was doing my usual thing, traveling to other planets and rescuing people, when Gus dared me to ride my bike down the big dirt hill in the open lot next to my house. He said I was too sissy to ride it.

I told him I rode down that hill several times a day, and it was no big deal. But his response was eerily like the challenge that Satan posed to Jesus in the wilderness: "Then why don't you prove it to me? I'll believe it when I see it."

That was my first mistake: taking the bait. I had never ridden my bike to prove anything to anyone and had no reason to start now. The boy on the bike was known to God, and that was enough. But unlike Jesus, I've always been inclined to say yes whenever someone asks me to prove something. So of course I indulged Gus. I took my bike to the top of the hill, got the fastest start I could muster, and went sailing down at maximum velocity. What I didn't know was that Gus had tied fishing wire tightly between two trees at the bottom of the hill. When I hit that line at top speed, the boy on the bike became the boy who could fly. I went soaring through the air in one direction, while my bike went soaring in the other. As I crashed to the ground, now squalling, with the fishing wire having dug deeply into my leg, the scene of my greatest creativity and innocence, the place where I was most open to God and to the world, became the scene of the crime.

Obviously, I survived my first encounter with a bully, and I lived to encounter many more. Some of those times were at the Bible camp I attended for three weeks every summer. I first started going to camp when I was twelve years old, which was younger than most of the kids, and it was during my turtleneck/fuzzy sweater/gold-chain-and-glasses phase, which meant, for all intents and purposes, I was asking to get beat up.

Bible camp was also where I was introduced to an entire culture of religious-oriented pranking. We were quite pre-occupied with the Rapture in those days, looking for our escape from the world, so the baseline prank was for everyone to sneak out of the cabin while the intended victim was still asleep or in the shower, leaving various assortments of clothes and shoes and underwear strewn around as if the Lord had returned and carried us away—buck naked, I guess. If all went as planned, when the target woke up or came out of the shower, he would think he had been "left behind" to face the Antichrist alone in the world.

One summer, we took turns making each other pass out. (Not a real bright idea, as we now know.) The guys did that to a friend of mine and then quickly dumped him into a dorm room with the lights out. When he woke up and saw the amber light from the hallway underneath the door and heard the sounds of the boys laughing maniacally, he thought he had died and gone to hell.

It was an environment in which there was a lot of talk about Satan and spiritual warfare. So, inevitably, the guys would single someone out and try to convince him he was under attack by demons. They'd break into his room, make a pentagram of salt on the floor, turn his Bible to page 666—that kind of thing. Then they'd hide down the hall until he came to his room. In the classic case, the boy took one look at his room and took off running in the other direction, screaming "Demons . . . DEMONS!" (If only the legion we've been talking about so far were as conspicuous as that sort of summer camp devil mythology, the world would be a much simpler place to navigate.)

For my part, I was given some of the most serious and potentially life-altering wedgies in the history of Bible camps everywhere, including the atomic wedgie, where they pull your underwear until the band breaks away from the fabric. The older kids often penny-locked me in my room. (If you don't already know how to do this, I'm not going to explain it to you and be held accountable for the trauma inflicted on another twelve-year-old boy.) Once they even duct-taped me to a chair *and* penny-locked me in my room.

I know such stories aren't unique to me. Everyone knows what it is to be bullied, to be displaced, to be labeled, to be left out. Yet what would it mean to have a God who had experienced all of those things?

The God who was bullied

We have always been inclined to worship people or things we perceive as being great. So we exaggerate our own greatness, inflate our successes, downplay our weaknesses, and hide our scars. Thus human history is largely the story of people who say, "My god can beat up your god, my king can beat up your king, my army is more awesome than your army," and then attempt to prove the point to each other. All in the name of greatness. In ancient cultures, people often tried to appeal to the extraordinary power and dominance of their gods as reasons for worship. Pharaohs, caesars, emperors, and even many of our contemporary celebrities are humans whose feats of power and achievement make people worship them as virtual gods.

So what do we make of a God who is worshipped not for His might but for His weakness, even for His wounds? Not a human wearing the medals of military conquest to convince us He is a god, but a God who wears His suffering on His sleeve to convince us He is human? Instead of "my god can beat up your god, my king can beat up your king," Jesus' path to kingship comes wrapped in a very odd strategy indeed: He is the King of kings largely because He lets himself get beat up. He is victorious not despite His scars, but because of them.

This is exactly what we are offered in Jesus—the God who was completely human, the one who demonstrated that He is the ultimate King by allowing Himself to be bullied. It is not only the songs of David that are embodied in Jesus of Nazareth, but also the song of the suffering servant recorded in Isaiah 53. These are the lyrics that reveal Jesus as an unattractive Messiah: "He had no form or majesty that we should look at him, nothing in his appearance that we should desire him" (Isaiah 53:2). These are the lyrics that reveal Jesus as an outcast, a man from the margins: "He was despised and rejected by others" (Isaiah 53:3). The song of Isaiah depicts the Messiah as a man who knew deep, abiding sadness on a first-name basis—"a man of sorrows, and acquainted with grief" (Isaiah 53:3, ESV). He was a human accustomed to rejection, "and as one from whom others hide their faces he was despised, and we held him of no account" (Isaiah 53:3). He was a man who knew what it meant to be completely abandoned by God and by humanity: "We accounted him stricken, struck down by God, and afflicted" (Isaiah 53:4). He was a man who even suffered injustice without making a case for Himself: "He was oppressed, and he was afflicted, yet he did not open his mouth; like a lamb that is led to the slaughter, and like a sheep that before its shearers is silent, so he did not open his mouth. By a perversion of justice he was taken away" (Isaiah 53:7-8).

The great reversal

The path to human power and influence, then and now, has always required that we conceal our scars, cover our wounds, and overcome the power of violence with greater violence. Yet the strange story of how Jesus became King inverts that entire order—by revealing His scars, exposing His wounds, and overcoming the power of violence by allowing the violent to overcome Him. This is exactly what the apostle Paul says happened when Jesus seemed to allow the principalities and powers—the ultimate bullying forces rolled up into one—to kill Him. Through the Cross, according to Colossians 2:15, "He disarmed the rulers and authorities and made a public example of them, triumphing over them."

When I was a kid, my favorite movie was *Superman II*. That's the one from 1980 in which Superman takes on three super villains (General Zod, Non, and Ursa) who have come to Earth from his native planet of Krypton, having all the same powers that he does. But early in the movie, Superman decides to renounce his superpowers so he can be with the woman he loves, Lois Lane. So he goes into a chamber back at his Fortress of Solitude (work with me here), and it turns him from Superman into plain old ordinary Clark Kent. Later in the film, after he finds out the super villains are running amok, Clark returns to the chamber and gets his powers back.

Spoiler alert: The climax of the film is a big fight in Metropolis between Superman and the evil trinity of superpowers. After trading blows with them there, Superman lures them back to the Fortress of Solitude, where they learn from Lex Luthor about the secret chamber. Having taken Lois Lane hostage, they tell Superman they will kill her if he doesn't surrender his power. Dejected but hopelessly in love with her, he agrees. We see the lights come on in the Fortress of Solitude—just like they did earlier in the film—and it appears that Superman has once again sacrificed his powers.

When the lights go off, and Superman is told to "bow and kneel before Zod," he gets down on one knee and bows his head. When Zod offers his hand, Superman takes it—lightly at first—and then begins to squeeze. We watch a look of terror come over Zod's face; we hear the bones in his hand snap. Superman gets up, lifting Zod over his head and discarding him like a piece of trash. It is only then that we realize what has happened—that somehow Superman has reversed the rays from the energy chamber, and while it looked like he was losing, he was actually winning all along.

It may be a crude analogy, but it is more or less what happened in the torture and death of Jesus on the cross. When He offered His own life up for the world, He turned that horrible weapon of imperial terror that the Roman Empire used to intimidate its citizens into the enduring symbol of love, hope, and forgiveness. By allowing His own life to be taken, Jesus exposed the pitiful "power" of the bullies and disarmed it. They thought they were making a spectacle out of Jesus, when in fact the Cross made a public spectacle out of them.

The book of Revelation gives us this same scene from a cosmic perspective, an aerial view of what Jesus accomplished on the cross. Because John's apocalypse uses war imagery, people often mistakenly assume that somehow the victory of God was incomplete on the cross, that the real victory comes when Jesus arrives with a sword and finally fights fire with fire, finally overcomes force with even greater force. But a careful reading shows that that is far from the case. For example, when Jesus comes riding in on a white horse with a sword, wearing a robe dipped in blood, it is not the blood of his opponents—it's His own. There is no battle scene, because Jesus has already defeated the powers (and all the bullies) through His sacrifice on the cross.

Blake's story

When we have suffered profoundly, we are given something much better than answers for "why." We are given the presence of a God who suffers and who makes His own wounds a resource for our healing.

When Blake Blackman worked behind the counter at the Common Market Deli, I thought she was a delight. She was friendly and funny. She cussed like a sailor but you couldn't help but like her. We were in our first year of Renovatus and had just started renting a little office in Charlotte's eclectic Plaza Midwood neighborhood. My friend Dennis Donahue, an elder in our church, often went with me for lunch at the Common Market, and he talked to Blake all the time. One Saturday, she needed help moving a piano, so Dennis and I helped out with that.

Dennis is sixtyish, in the real estate business, and quite possibly the most genuinely funny human being I know. We didn't go to the Common Market like missionaries looking to convert everyone. We simply believed that God had called us to love the people in our neighborhood really well, and that was the entirety of our agenda. No tracts, no prepared spiels, no crib sheets of Christian apologetics, no politely listening to people finish their sentences while frothing for the opportunity to tell them the "plan of salvation."

I had been moved by John Wesley's line "The world is my parish" and had decided I was the pastor of everyone in my neighborhood, whether they acknowledged me as such or not. I didn't need their permission to love them like mad, listen to their stories, or be their friend. And what else exactly is a pastor supposed to do? I believed then, as I do now, that if Jesus really is the prototype for a whole new way of being human, and His way of functioning in the world is as revolutionary as I believe it is, if we will just show up, He'll take care of the heavy lifting. I didn't believe I needed to "bring God with me" into Plaza Midwood, because one of my baseline assumptions about ministry is that God is *already* wherever I'm headed, and I'm just there to help folks recognize Him. Dennis and I loved our friends, and we believed God's presence was strongly with us in the same way He's present whenever anybody really loves someone.

I was glad that Blake didn't know I was a pastor, because I liked her saltiness (then and now) and it would have been sad if she tried to conceal it. Eventually, of course, we arrived at the fateful day when she asked me what I did for a living. When I told her, she was mortified—remember, she was wearing her trademark "God is my co-pirate"

T-shirt—which was precisely the response I didn't want.
I liked Blake's personality too much and was convinced
(then and now) that Jesus enjoys her spitfire personality.

I didn't know anything about the journey she had been
on. I didn't know she had lost her one-year-old son, Zyler,
eight years before, when he went into cardiac arrest after a
successful surgery to repair two holes in his heart. I didn't
know about her divorce a year later. Or the string of
unhealthy relationships she'd had with other men before
meeting her boyfriend, Jason. Or her failed experiments at
developing a spiritual side, including a season in which she
tried Buddhism. I didn't know about the difficulties her
eight-year-old son, Noah, was having that year in school.

Blake could be snarky, but she was charismatic and always
charming, and beneath her big personality she had never let
her story out in my direction. In Blake's words, she didn't
have a relationship with God, and yet when Zyler died and
her husband left, she decided she hated Him. Whenever
religion came up at the Common Market, Blake told everybody it was all a farce and that God was a jerk.

Several weeks after the conversation about my occupa-
tion, on a morning when a storm of emotions was raging
inside her, Blake was standing over a box at the Common
Market, aggressively slapping price tags onto bottles of
wine. The whole time, she later told me, she was talking in
her head—which she now recognizes as praying, though
she didn't know it at the time—saying something like
this: *Okay, listen: I am miserable. I don't know what to do*

anymore. I have tried everything. I have been to grief counseling, I have read self-help books; I even tried Buddhism for a while. I don't know what else there is out there to fix this. But I want to get better. I want to help Noah get better. I will do absolutely anything. Just tell me what to do!

At that moment, she straightened up to put the wine on a shelf. Just beyond the wine shelves were some drink coolers with sodas and water. As she placed a bottle on the shelf, she glanced over and saw me standing at the cooler getting a bottle of water. Instantly, she was overcome with intense anger. She hated God and the very idea that this could be some sort of "sign" that she was supposed to talk to a Christian pastor was out of the question.

She stood arguing with herself for what she said felt like an eternity. *No, no, NO. I am not going to walk over there.* But at that point, she felt so miserable that she was willing to try anything. Deciding to take the risk, she asked if she could talk to me. (She now claims that it was with a smart mouth and sassy attitude, but it didn't feel that way to me at the time.) So that afternoon at two o'clock, she and I sat down in my office and she told me her story.

For ninety minutes, she spilled her guts: about her ex-husband, Zyler's death, her bad experiences with church when she was young, her hatred for God. She said she saw God as an entity up in the heavens who operated all of us like marionettes, orchestrating our lives for His own entertainment—and that He laughed at us like one would laugh at a movie.

I let Blake do almost all of the talking that day. When she got done unleashing her seething anger at God, I asked her, "Well, have you told Him any of that?"

"Him who?"

"God. Have you told God all the things you've just told me?"

She looked at me like I was crazy. She told me later she had two reactions: (1) If God is God, surely He knows all of this; and (2) You can't talk to God like that. You can talk *about* Him, but not *to* Him—at least not like that. (This was her reaction even though she didn't like God and had no relationship with Him.)

I took her to some places in the Psalms of David where the music gets dark and dissonant, where David feels abandoned and forsaken and his prayers take on a tone of accusation. I told her that's why those Psalms are there, so we'd know how to talk to God when we were feeling the same way. I did not feel the least bit inclined to explain to Blake that she was a sinner or ask her to repeat after me to ask Jesus into her heart. I could feel the ache of God for her, and I knew that if she even cracked the door open to Him in an honest conversation, He'd take it from there.

Blake acted appreciative to me, but she told me later she left feeling as cynical as she had going in. I had come nowhere near to giving Blake an answer for why her life had taken such miserable turns. I did not believe God was responsible for any of it, because my understanding of God is nothing like the image of manipulating marionettes for entertainment. In any case, I was not pretentious enough even then to try to broker an explanation for God. I know much less about why God allows people to suffer than I know that He Himself is a suffering God. There is something implicitly understood that public personalities in general, and preachers in particular, feel the need to have an authoritative position on everything. I myself have never been able to trust people who speak authoritatively about everything.

When Jesus' best friend, Lazarus, dies, it seems like an opportune moment to speak the unspeakable, to bring clarity to the haze of grief. Instead, in one of the most wrenching scenes in Scripture, Jesus delays His arrival in Bethany for four days. *Four days.* When He finally shows up, all eyes are on the prophet/sage/master/teacher, the wisest of the wise, awaiting a word that will heal, a word that will explain, a word that will comfort. If there is anything we might rightly expect from the man who delivered the Sermon on the Mount, it would be the gift of words. And yet with the weight of expectation towering over Him, those closest to Lazarus are given the gift of God's wordlessness. The answer they receive is the contorted face of Jesus—and hot tears. There was nothing to be said. It was a time for grief, not for answers.

Sometimes, the sacred thing, the wise thing, the compassionate thing, the best thing, the anointed thing, is simply to *shut up.* I learned a long time ago that there are some things in life so dark that if an answer is asked for, the only reply we are able to give is our tears or our presence. Sometimes the best response is in the courage and wisdom to say, "I don't know," but then don't walk away. Some questions are not opportunities; they're temptations—to play God, to play the expert, to play doctor, to build a platform or a reputation.

If there is anything that would scare me, it would be to utter words in a scenario where God Himself would not speak. All I knew was that if Blake spewed her anguish in God's direction, she might not get an answer, but she would be guaranteed to experience the God who suffers. I knew that the song of the suffering servant is the song that absorbs all of our weeping into its dissonant melody.

Blake didn't feel any better at first. But over the next few days, she kept thinking about what I had said. About a week later, she was home alone and still feeling out of sorts. It was a nice day. She had the front and back doors open and began pacing the house and taking laps around the backyard as she rehashed our conversation almost verbatim. She started telling God how she felt. She got mad, cussed, told Him she hated Him, that He had ruined her life. She said her life was a mess, and she didn't think she was ever going to get it back on track. She told God that He owed her. He had taken everything from her and she expected Him to give it back. She continued to pace the house, yelling and cussing for over an hour. Every feeling she had, she let out, her anger punctuated by tears.

"When I was done," she said, "even though it sounds

supernatural and weird, I literally felt something break. It wasn't exactly like peace, but like the things inside of me that had been weighing me down broke into smaller pieces. Instead of being pressed down, something lifted, and I was able to breathe again. I could tell right away something was different."

Blake knew she was far from being well, but *something* had happened. From there, she started actively thinking about coming to Renovatus. Three weeks later, after reluctantly asking her boss for a Sunday off work, she showed up. She was terrified. She was a twenty-nine-year-old single mom with an eight-year-old kid, and she knew enough about Bible Belt churches to wonder if she would be judged when she walked through the door.

The first few weeks, she arrived as late as she could, anxiously smoking one last cigarette to brace herself before she came inside. "Deep down," she said, "I thought you would all be hypocrites. I wanted to be able to point and laugh and say, 'You're all wrong.' But everybody treated me like I was important to them, like they wanted to spend time with me. And this was not done under the guise of evangelism. Not one person made me feel like they wanted to save me. They just wanted to love me. It was so countercultural to what I'd been experiencing. I had never been part of a community where people seemed to be looking out for someone else's good rather than their own. I was so broken. I needed that love and attention so bad. I couldn't walk away from it."

She admitted to being a little freaked out by the music and the people who raised their hands while they were singing. She didn't know what to expect from the sermons, but she said, "I could feel in my body that what Jonathan was saying was the truth."

She had never before in her life heard anything like the way I described the Kingdom of God, who the people of God are, and how they participate in the world. She said, "But when you talked, I could tell that you were speaking what God would say. If God had to describe what His Kingdom was like, I think this is how He would describe it."

Blake said she had always felt like a victim of broken systems. "You would be talking about the ways we marginalize and oppress each other and try to get a leg up so we can look good and gain whatever it is we need. I've always felt like that—like I've been operating in a world that's not worth operating in. It's not working. It's broken. People treat each other bad because of it. It's not right and good that someone just tells me what to do. So when you were explaining what the Kingdom of God looks like, lightbulbs went on for me. I thought, *This is what the world is supposed to be like! Why wouldn't you want to be a part of this? Why wouldn't you want to get your identity from God instead of this world and the awful things it has to offer?*

Gradually, she stopped feeling as if she needed to scratch and claw to get to a place that's good. She realized she was already there, because God was there. She said God healed her through the teaching at Renovatus and the people who came alongside her, loving and hugging and not giving up on her. "I realized there really is an alternative to the horribleness of this world. It's a broken, scary, messy place. I don't have to live there anymore, so now I don't."

A few months later, Blake asked me for permission to start a support group at Renovatus for people who had suffered tragedy like she had. We were thrilled. She went from hating God to becoming a wounded healer for other people in our community who needed to experience the presence of God, familiar with grief in the way that she was. Two years later, when we moved into the dilapidated old theater at Eastland Mall, Blake quit her job and asked for permission to raise her own support to do ministry in the mall. Instead of working the counter at the Common Market, Blake set up a café in the lobby where she served free coffee and snacks just to build relationships with people in the mall. Day after day, they would come and sit for hours, spilling their guts to Blake the way that she had that day in my office. And it was precisely through efforts like these that people like my friend Casim found their way into our church.

See how it works? God finds us in obscurity, but also raises us up to bring comfort to others. Blake is one of many in our community who has followed Jesus as the prototype for a new way to be human. Rather than hiding His scars, Jesus made His own brokenness a resource for healing for the entire world. Like Him, Blake is now a wounded healer who makes her own wounds available to other people who are suffering.

Sally's story

There is no wound so grotesque that it cannot become a resource for healing. That's the way of the future. The world we live in tells us to hide our scars, to pretend we are stronger and more beautiful than we are. The new world God is creating through us is one in which scars are displayed like merit badges instead of hidden under makeup. We don't conceal our scars because our scars are our story, and our story, however broken, is a story of the tenderness of God.

My friend Sally Tolentino, a leader in our church, was a missionary for many years in the Dominican Republic. But it wasn't until she was in her sixties that she began to come to terms with the sexual abuse she had experienced at the hands of two members of her family, as well as a former pastor. At a Sunday morning worship service last year, this mother in the faith shared her story publicly for the first time. For her to share her scars and her displacement in such an open way has made it safe for other abused women to share their brokenness too. We have heard one remarkable story after another from daughters and sisters and wives who have experienced healing from the wounds of sexual abuse through the weekly support group Sally leads, called The King's Daughters.

Several months ago at Renovatus, at the end of a sermon, I gave an invitation for anyone in our body to come forward for prayer who had had significant authority figures in their lives either abuse them or withhold affection from them. Our leaders lined across the front of the room, ready to anoint them with oil as a symbol of the presence of the Holy Spirit. It is a terrible thing to ask someone who has been touched harmfully to be open to redemptive touch. We knew that, after years of suffering, one prayer would not be enough to make it all better. But we also believed that exposing those wounds before God and before others could at least begin a process of healing. Nevertheless, it still felt almost irresponsible to ask for such a complex bomb of human emotions to be released in that room on a Sunday morning. I stood on the stage and witnessed a mass unleashing of human anguish mixed with pent-up fury a few feet in front of me, as sons and daughters were embraced by mothers and fathers in the Lord. As the scene unfolded, I thought to myself, *This is it. We have crossed the line. This is entirely too holy.*

Part of our task as new humans is that we do not dismiss the sons or daughters who have been abused, but learn to weep with them, learn to embrace them. We repent of our neglect of their stories of pain and humiliation, as well as any part we have played in perpetuating their pain. We remember again our wounded healer, Jesus, whose wounds are the source of such great healing for all of our own.

We behold the scars of our brothers and sisters, despised

and rejected of men, acquainted with grief. We refuse to hide our faces from those who were despised, those who at one time we did not esteem. We behold the one who was wounded for our transgressions, bruised for our iniquities. By His stripes . . . we are healed.[2] In a reality that may seem perfectly horrible to you, especially if you have been victimized in this way, somehow both the abused and the abusers are able to be reconciled at the foot of the cross of Christ. I do not understand this, but I can bear witness to it. When the prototype for a new humanity died on the cross, the possibilities for both victims and victimizers to be swept up in new creation sprang open. That is why even the splendor and terror of Mount Sinai, where Moses encountered the dazzling fire and smoke of God's literal presence, could never be more holy than the hill on which Jesus died.

The blessing and the limp

As the prototype for a new way of being human, and as the one who awakens us to our true selves, Jesus shows us how our scars can become a resource for healing instead of a source of shame. That's not to say that whenever we bring our suffering to Jesus, everything is easily or magically healed and we will never feel the pain again. But it does mean that even in the darkest moments there is yet a blessing—a deep revelation of our belovedness that is as profound as the hurt that we feel.

We catch a glimpse of this strange mixture of pain and blessing in Genesis 32:22-32, one of the most enigmatic passages in the Bible. Jacob has a mysterious encounter with an angel, and he wants a blessing from him. In order to get it, he wrestles with the angel all night long. When the dawn breaks, Jacob has the blessing he was looking for, but he also has a dislocated hip. By clinging desperately to the angel throughout a tumultuous dark night of the soul, Jacob got what was he looking for. But he also walked away with a permanent limp.

I'm more convinced than ever of God's generosity, of the ways He delights to give good gifts to His children. But if we wrestle with God and walk away with a blessing, the blessing won't be the only thing that marks us. There will still be dried blood and unsightly bruises and hips that don't quite work the way they used to that come from the long night of wrestling. Gifts come without strings attached, but that's not to say they come without consequences. It's why so many people go through their lives keeping their greatest blessings at arm's length. They may intrinsically know that blessing is on the other side of struggle, that relief and comfort are on the other side of the dark night, but they don't want to risk the suffering in order to get there.

If fear makes you want to stay home, you're in good company. Many strong and competent people have chosen the path of least resistance, deciding it is better to walk away without bruises or broken bones. They have pragmatically decided it is better to keep the safer blessings they have than take the risk of having to stare down God, the devil, and themselves. And make no mistake, the dark night of the soul will involve wrestling with all three. In the midst of it, you really don't know if you're going to make it to sunup.

It sounds so sterile and truncated to narrate the tale even now: "Jacob wrestled with an angel all night." It sounds so straightforward, so uncomplicated. But how could wrestling with an angel be uncomplicated? Night complicates most everything to begin with. And don't you know how long a night can feel? The way time seems to slow down? In the middle of the night, fevers rise and hopes plummet. If it feels like our lives are in perpetual fast-forward sometimes, sleepless nights feel like an endless instant replay—with fear and regret in super slo-mo. Given all that, it is difficult to judge anybody too harshly for wanting to avoid something as terrible as having to stare down God and his own demons. I understand all too well the desire to avoid bruising.

And yet there is still the reality of blessing, the promise that lies on the other side—that if you just don't let go, the blessing will be as extravagant as the night is long, and the bliss as sweet as the night is painful. It isn't necessary to *win*, only to not lose hold of the one with whom we're wrestling. Blessedness is a feast that can be savored only by those who have first tasted their own blood.

When you've been wrestling all night for a blessing, it might be difficult to say you would do it all over again when the dawn breaks. Being glad you didn't let go—that you hung on for dear life—is not the same as saying you'd volunteer for it again. Still, you can't escape the truth that the sacredness of your life has been enhanced by both the blessing and by the wrestling itself. That's what gratitude feels like.

The truth is, blessings that come without bruises and victories that come without a limp as a souvenir won't be particularly sweet or memorable. Granted, there is a lingering soreness inherent in a night of wrestling. It's true that long after the night is over, the slightest movement may trigger a familiar pain. But with the wince of the wound comes the visceral reminder of blessedness.

What a fascinating phenomenon: Every time Jacob stepped awkwardly, you couldn't tell if he was wincing or smiling. Maybe it was both. After his night in the wilderness, every step carried the message of blessedness and belovedness. To have that message seared into your joints may well be worth a thousand years of dark nights.

In short, if you have no limp, you likely have no blessing. At the very least, without a limp you are less aware of the blessings you have, which might be just as bad. At this point, I am far more inclined to think that walking with a limp but knowing the blessing is decidedly better than walking whole without the blessing.

If you are in the midst of a long night of wrestling, there are no strategies or steps I could give you to make it end faster. But strategy is not required—perseverance is. You wouldn't remember steps if I gave them to you, not when the night gets really dark and long. But do remember this much: *Don't stop until the sun is up.* And remember that the reason for the wrestling is not because God is out to kill you, but that He has really wanted to bless you all along. You don't have to do anything to *earn* the blessing—in fact, you can't; you can't be strong enough or powerful enough. You just have to stay in the ring, and the dawn that creeps up when the wrestling is over will take care of the rest.

> Weeping may endure for a night,
> but joy comes in the morning. (Psalm 30:5, NKJV)

> Then he said, "Let me go, for the day is breaking." But Jacob said, "I will not let you go, unless you bless me." (Genesis 32:26)

6

resurrection

✧ ✧ ✧

Everything dies, baby, that's a fact,
But maybe everything that dies someday comes back.

BRUCE SPRINGSTEEN,
"ATLANTIC CITY"

As I often do, I woke up one morning from a dream about the house my grandmother lived in. My grandparents retired in the 1970s and moved to the old Church of God campground in Charlotte, North Carolina, where our denomination's state office was. It was the site of the tabernacle where we had our sweaty Pentecostal camp meetings every July (these were like weeklong revivals where all our churches got together). As far as I was concerned, it was the center of the entire universe. It was where I went to Bible camp in the summer. It was where I had all my first experiences, from the Holy Ghost to my first kiss (not necessarily in that order).

It was an enormous, sprawling property, with houses all around the perimeter that were built for aging Church of God preachers to retire to. My grandfather was one of those preachers. He was a hard man who grew up in Charlotte and later became a police officer. When he met the beautiful Nellie Edwards, he knew he had to have her as his own. But she would hear nothing of it. "I don't date sinner boys," she told him.

That's how S. D. Martin ended up in an old-time holiness revival service at the Parkwood Church of God. And sure enough, he got saved, sanctified, and full of the Holy Ghost. A few weeks later, he turned in his badge and gun, telling his captain that God called him to preach—though he hadn't booked a single revival yet. That's how S. D. and Nellie became "Brother and Sister Martin" and ended up pastoring in rural North Carolina churches in places like Rutherfordton and Shelby. God was the one who did all the saving, mind you, but it's no surprise that Nellie was more or less the reason a man like S. D. would be willing to change the course of his entire life; she was just that strong of a woman. Years later when they retired, they settled into a nice little house at the back of the Church of God campground overlooking the big pond.

My earliest memory in life is of my grandfather walking me down to that pond, where he used to fish. I remember my mom being upset because I was wearing new white shoes she had bought me and I got mud on them. A few days later, Grandpa died of a heart attack on that very property, working in his garden behind the house.

With Grandpa gone, I spent most of my summers alone with my grandmother at that house. This predates the boy on the bike. Everything about that place was magical to me. We watched *The Price Is Right* every day and then played Scrabble. She made Tang and fried cornbread. I can remember everything about her and the house and her little poodle, Fiji.

I have had many wonderful people in my life, but nobody like my grandmother—the way she loved me and the way she talked about Jesus and taught me about life. When my dad was preaching in different churches on the weekends, she would come with us when she could, and they always asked Sister Martin to testify. Whether or not the service was going well before that, it caught fire when she spoke, because there was an electricity and a tremble in her voice that said this was a woman who knew God in ways the rest of us just didn't. Anybody who ever heard her testify or preach will tell you the same thing—that the hairs on the back of their neck stood up when she talked about Jesus. She was the most tender, genuine person I have ever known. There was no way I could not have believed in God, because I believed in my grandmother. I couldn't have made sense of her if her God didn't exist. It's as simple as that.

Today those old grounds look like the perfect set for a horror movie. Everything is overgrown, and though the big building that housed the tabernacle still stands, much of it collapsed in a fire years ago. Every so often I sneak under the fence, trespass onto the grounds, and walk through the sacred sites now covered with graffiti and littered with drug paraphernalia. The only way I can ever really go back is in my dreams. They are all different and yet they are all the same. This morning, I woke up dreaming I was carrying my goddaughter up the hill to show her the pond, but we couldn't get through because the road was too overgrown. She was wearing white shoes too. I have had these dreams since my grandmother died, always either going back to the house or trying to get back to it.

And why wouldn't I want to go back? I don't write about wounds and limping and heartache as a dispassionate bystander. I've lived long enough to have scars of my own, long enough to be disappointed with life, and long enough most of all to be disappointed with myself. Who wouldn't want to go back? That urban jungle of overgrowth on Wilkinson Boulevard was the Garden of Eden to me. It's where I walked with God naked and unashamed. I love Jesus on His own terms, I suppose, but in a sense He's always been my grandmother's Jesus, and that's the only one I'd care to know. What would I know about Him without her? She drew me to Him no less than she drew S. D. in the 1920s.

I think most of what you need to know about how life with God works is probably wrapped up in the bittersweet taste of dreams. All that longing and aching for something beautiful that is just out of reach. Sometimes you can touch it and sometimes you can't. Everything in you that longs for beauty and music comes alive in those dreams, and for a moment you are the *you* that once was, before wounds and scars and choices and consequences and disappointment took their toll. You can practically taste the innocence and wonder before you knew too much, saw too much, felt too much. By the time you grasp for it, you wake up to the world that has long since moved on. Not that the world as it is doesn't have beauty of its own, but how could it compare to the life you had before your scars? For a moment, you thought you could go back, but there is no going back. People die, hopes and dreams die, and weeds grow where wonder once lived. These days, bicycles and trampolines aren't time machines so much. What is done is done, what is lost is lost.

Unless . . . what if it were still possible to go back? What if death really wasn't the final word on the people we love the most? What if cancer and car accidents and closed caskets weren't the end after all? What if instead of being snatched out of the dream while our hands are still grasping, it were possible to actually reach out and touch those people again? Not to just imagine their touch or remember their voice, but to actually touch them and trace the lines on their face, feel the hair on their arms, feel their hot and living breath on your skin?

If you're like me, to even think of such a thing stirs an ache and longing deep enough to make you double over if you entertain it for long. But of course such a thing is impossible. Isn't that what makes death so terrible—the finality of it? Isn't that what makes it so awful? It's the thing that can't ever be undone. There is nothing as terrible as death.

Which is why for death to be undone, it would take something more terrible still.

The worst thing that could happen

Nothing is as fearful as death. Nothing is as terrible as the moment when you lower a loved one into the ground and cover the casket with earth. Nothing makes time stand still quite like death—except for resurrection, that is. Except for the earth opening up and the dead coming back to life.

In Matthew's Gospel, the language about Jesus' death is curiously apocalyptic. The world that had seemed so charged with beauty while God walked in the flesh now turns into a George Romero film.

"Darkness came over the whole land" (Matthew 27:45). The dark music of Psalms is the only thing left for Jesus. He cries out in the ancient tongue, "*'Eli, Eli, lema sabach-thani?'* that is, 'My God, my God, why have you forsaken me?'" (Matthew 27:46). And when the music dies, the earth itself quivers in terror. Rocks are split and tombs are opened.

Three days later, the unthinkable happens. The Spirit of music animates the body of the crucified God, and He walks out of the tomb where they had buried Him. It is not an apparition and it is not a dream. His friends know this because He still has the scars.

In perhaps the most unheralded verse in the New Testament, when Jesus is resurrected, there is a moment in which the world itself seems to blink, and in an instant the world is something different than it was before: "The tombs also were opened, and many bodies of the saints who had fallen asleep were raised. After his resurrection they came out of the tombs and entered the holy city and appeared to many" (Matthew 27:52-53). It's the first Easter, but there are no bunnies and no one is wearing pastels. It's like a zombie apocalypse without anyone being eaten. There is something beautiful about all of this, to be sure, but if you find it simply comforting, you're not thinking about it hard enough.

People so often live in fear of the worst-case scenario. What if I lost the person I love most in the world to a tragic accident? What if there is another 9/11? What if there is a nuclear war? The good and bad news is this: The worst thing that could ever happen has already happened. God died! The Son of Love entered into His own creation, bringing tenderness and beauty and goodness to everything and everybody He touched. But our eyes had seen far too much at that point to recognize beauty when we saw it, so we did not recognize Him. And the most hopeful thing that had ever happened to the world fell into the same hole where all our hopes and dreams and loved ones must ultimately fall—the grave.

But the terror of death was overcome by something more

terrible yet in resurrection. After the worst thing that could ever happen happened, love climbed back out of the abyss. Don't you see that if it happened to Jesus, it is a bigger story than one man rising from the dead? The reason there is a moment when the world seems to have gone all to hell—or all to heaven or whatever you want to call it—is because resurrection changes everything. If that man could get up, anybody could get up. If hope died and came back to life, then hope can rise again for the whole world. If even God can die but come back to life, then anyone can come back to life.

In these verses, for a few fleeting moments, we catch a glimpse not just of Jesus, but of where the entire world is headed. People saw their heroes and loved ones walking around for an instant just like Jesus was. If it is true that Jesus rose from the dead . . . well, life will never be quite the same again.

It is hard to imagine anything more momentous than God rising from the dead, but what if that was just the trailer and not the movie? What if it means that the Garden of Eden isn't really gone (and maybe even the Church of God campground, in my case) and that the people we've lost aren't really gone forever? What if there really is a way back? Though we, like Jesus, will still have the scars we've picked up along the way, what if we could get up like He did? What if nothing that seems lost is really lost?

You can see how the Resurrection wasn't just about Jesus' rising—as essential to the whole process as it was.

The world convulsed, and in the seizure we saw the world not as it is but as it would one day become.

Doubt

Who wouldn't want to believe such a thing? Who wouldn't want it to be true—that one Man could rise from the dead, and because of that one moment when the world was turned on its ear, the day will one day come when corpse after corpse will follow Him, reassembled, reconfigured. And (this part may surprise you) what if the idea is not that He will lead them off to a place far, far away to a magic kingdom full of fairies and gold dust but that the departed people we have loved will actually come back to the places where we loved them, and we can have it all back? There is a reason that so many people have believed this over the centuries and that so many more have wanted to: It's just that good!

But it is precisely because it is so good that many people can't bring themselves to believe it—it sounds too good to be true. Every one of us knows what it feels like to get our hopes up about something we care about deeply, only to have them dashed against the rocks. We have fallen and cracked our heads open against the hard corners of reality. We aren't surprised anymore when we are disappointed. And let's not speak too piously now—we've also been the source of someone else's crushing disappointment. We've let others down, just as we've been let down. We aren't just bruised, we've done the bruising.

Aren't we a little too old for fairy tales? Now that we know that nobody lives happily ever after (least of all ourselves), wouldn't it be better to attach ourselves to something a bit more pragmatic than Middle Eastern folk literature? Wouldn't we be better off taking inspiration from the essentially human longing inherent in the tale, but no more so than we would from, say, *The Lord of the Rings*, *The NeverEnding Story*, or Greek mythology? Of course it's a good story—and wouldn't it be great if it were true?—but we have to get back to the real world. We've been disappointed too many times to dare get our hopes up again. We already know how *that* story is going to end.

This is not a new problem. Jesus' disciples had given up three years of their lives to follow Him. He had turned their unremarkable lives into music with His symphony. They were beginning to teach and to touch and feel the same goodness that was in Him flow through their own lives. They believed He was the anointed one, the Messiah their prophets had foretold. And now everything they had hoped and believed had been laid to waste with the mangled body of Jesus of Nazareth. No wonder that when the women came back from the garden to tell the disciples the tomb was empty, it was so difficult to believe.

Thomas, famously, was the last holdout. You know this if you went to Sunday school because history has unfairly labeled him "doubting Thomas," as if one moment of his life summed up his entire character. Thomas was surely known to his friends for many other things. He may have been the disciple who always brought the coleslaw—"old coleslaw Thomas" to the other guys. To sum up a faithful and complex man as "doubting Thomas" for more than twenty centuries makes about as much sense as it would to call me "Wedgie Martin" for the rest of my life because of a bad Bible camp experience when I was twelve. But it is true that he doubted. The disciples told him, "We have seen the Lord" (John 20:24), but Thomas wanted to see for himself—it sounded too good to be true. So he said, "Unless I see the mark of the nails in his hands, and put my finger in the mark of the nails and my hand in his side, I will not believe" (John 20:25).

It's true that Thomas was a doubter, but he was not a cynic, and that's an important distinction. Cynics often look for reasons not to believe and won't be moved by something beautiful—just to make a point—even if it's staring them down. Thomas wasn't a cynic, he was a hopeful doubter; he'd believe if he could. He'd believe if it wasn't contingent on just *hearing* a story—he needed to touch with his fingertips. For him to believe, the message embedded in his nerves would have to travel to his brain to report, "He's really here."

Maybe you *are* cynical; if so, I have no judgment for you—I've been cynical too, toward God, the world, and myself. But do you know the feeling of hopeful doubting? Do you know what it's like to feel something in you that strains to believe, yearns to trust—if only there were a little bit of evidence?

The resurrected Jesus was no less tender with His hopeful disciples after He passed through the veil of death. He knew where Thomas's heart was:

> Jesus came and stood among them and said, "Peace be with you." Then he said to Thomas, "Put your finger here and see my hands. Reach out your hand and put it in my side. Do not doubt but believe." Thomas answered him, "My Lord and my God!" (John 20:26-28)

Jesus wasn't angry at Thomas. When Thomas so desperately needed to feel the wounds (which is how we know anyone is real, incidentally—when we can touch their wounds), Jesus offered His body to Thomas's probing, intrusive touch. If in order to believe, he needed to touch Jesus in the places where He was hurt, then okay.

Jesus is extraordinarily tender to doubters. There is another lovely scene in the Gospels, after His resurrection, when Jesus appears to His disciples. They are in the middle of an incredible existential crisis—*Our rabbi is dead and everything is lost and what are we going to do and what have the last three years been about, anyway?* It might seem as if Jesus would morph into flames and appear to them dramatically, like God did for Moses on Mount Sinai (or as the Holy Spirit would soon do for the disciples on Pentecost), when the light was so bright that you had to look away for fear of your life. Instead, Jesus' response is playful: "Why don't we eat some fish?"[1] The disciples are falling apart, and Jesus does the most reassuring, quintessentially human thing imaginable: He shares a meal with them. So basic, so elemental to human existence: "Let's you and me grab a bite to eat." The disciples want to solve their existential crisis; Jesus wants to have a fish sandwich.

It's no accident that, in another narrative, mealtime is when Jesus chooses to reveal Himself. Not long after the Crucifixion, two disciples encounter a stranger on the road to Emmaus, and they tell him how terrible the last few days have been. He plays dumb, and they are incredulous. "How could you not have heard what happened to Jesus of Nazareth? Don't you watch the news?"

It isn't until they take a break from all the walking and talking—"You've got a lot on your mind. Let's get off our feet for a few minutes and just relax; let's just be together"—and Jesus breaks bread for a meal, that the familiar gesture snaps the two disciples out of their spell: "Hey, that's Him! That's Jesus."[2]

Even after all the disciples have encountered the resurrected Jesus and He is about to ascend, Matthew's Gospel records a fascinating detail: "When they saw him, they worshiped him; *but some doubted*" (Matthew 28:17, emphasis added). Apparently, for some of Jesus' closest friends, even seeing Him in the flesh wasn't enough to dispel all of their doubts.

When we gather at Renovatus, we call it a "worship service," but we could more aptly say "worship and doubting service," because that's really what's always going on in the room.

I am no stranger to doubt. I understand Thomas all too well. My own need to touch and handle is often greater than my capacity to "just believe." There is a potent scene in John Patrick Shanley's play-turned-film, *Doubt*. The film tells the story of a priest (played by Philip Seymour Hoffman) who is accused of abusing a child. Throughout the film, the elder nun (played by Meryl Streep), who brings the accusation, is the only character who seems to have certainty. She seems always strong, confident, ever sure of herself, a stranger to ambiguity. In the film's final scene, however, as she sits on an outdoor bench beside a younger nun (played by Amy Adams), she finally breaks: "Oh, Sister . . . I have such *doubts!*"

Of course there are times, after cruising at the high altitudes of a sermon, when I project undiluted confidence—as if I'm the biggest personality in the room, opening up my trench coat and distributing assurance like lifted watches to everyone present—but actually I'm more ready to collapse on a park bench; times when the lurking doubt underneath the impenetrable surface threatens to flood out of me: "Oh, Sister . . . I have such doubts!"

But my doubts do not sum me up any more than they did Thomas. And my doubts are no reason for me not to follow Jesus. I follow Jesus not because I don't have any doubts. I follow Jesus because in my doubt, He has always been tender with me. And when I've needed it badly enough, He has always given me a body to touch.

A world we'd like to live in

The claim is not just that the resurrection of Jesus changes people—but that His resurrection power has already changed the world. The problem, of course, is that there are so many ways in which the world is still living in protest to its deepest calling. We don't have to look very far to see how much suffering and evil and injustice are still at work all around us. And yet when people really come to believe that Jesus has been raised from the dead and start to live their lives accordingly, we begin to see demonstrated what the new resurrected world looks like. As strange as it might sound, people begin to experience the reality of the Resurrection through our very ordinary lives. And people who live their lives in the power of the Resurrection—that is, living as people from the future—in a real sense begin to take responsibility for God in the world.

For most people, this is where faith in God begins. Rowan Williams, the former Archbishop of Canterbury, writes, "Belief in God starts . . . from a sense that we 'believe in,' we trust some kinds of people. We have confidence in the way they live; the way they live is a way I want to live, perhaps can imagine myself living in my better or more mature moments. The world they inhabit is one I'd like to live in. Faith has a lot to do with the simple fact that there are trustworthy lives to be seen, that we can see in some believing people a world we'd like to live in."[3]

Odd as it still seems for me now, Dennis Donahue and I were "trustworthy lives" for Blake Blackman. Long before anything changed in her life, she told me, she got excited when Dennis and I came in the door, but she didn't know why. She would come to work wondering if she would see us that day—which created some cognitive dissonance for her because she "hated Christians." She wasn't struck by anything we ever said about our faith—she was struck that we were always genuinely interested in her and how she was doing. She couldn't figure out why she felt so different after a conversation with us, compared to her interactions with other customers and friends.

She said when she talked to other folks at Common Market, she would leave the conversation feeling justified and right about all her negative feelings, about her sense that the world was out to get her. "We all thought we were relatively happy, as far as I know," Blake said. "We just had all the answers. We knew life's cruel secrets and the jig was up, in our opinion. You weren't going to get one over on us. We weren't going to be caught by surprise."

But when she had lunch with Dennis and me, she said, "I left feeling like there is so much more out there. And you knew what the 'so much more' was, and I didn't. You had something I wanted, but I certainly had no idea what that something was. It was one of the most curious and unexplainable things I had ever come up against. I know this sounds odd, and maybe even a little cheesy, but when I spent time with you guys, I felt the warmest and most normal I had felt in a long, long time. Again, totally cheesy, I know, but it was always as if there were some deep well of contentment that you two operated from. Of course, I had no way of articulating that at the time. I know I felt something emanating off of you, but I honestly didn't know what it was."

Years after my grandmother died, I came to know this feeling for myself through Sister Margaret Gaines, whom I call my spiritual grandmother. The week after Christmas last year, I was sleeping on a sofa hide-a-bed in Pell City, Alabama, when the delicate sounds of eighty-year-old Sister Margaret working quietly in the adjacent kitchen slowly awakened me. I was still in the hazy shadowland between dream and reality when I began to hear the pots and pans and her voice softly humming a hymn. She was trying not to wake me, but it was hardly a bother. When I'm at Margaret's house and she's making fresh Arab bread and hummus, the old Church of God campground doesn't seem nearly so out of reach. And when I share a meal with Sister Margaret, I always recognize something that gives me another reason to believe that Jesus has been raised from the dead after all. I wasn't able to touch the wounded body of Jesus, and now I can't wrap my arms around my grandmother, either. But in Sister Margaret, I've got a stand-in.

I didn't know Sister Margaret well until I was in my early twenties. I knew *about* her because she was famous in my denomination as a missionary. The first time I met with

Margaret, I literally cried for three hours as we talked, and was still so overcome by the time I left that I staggered to my car as if I were drunk. It wasn't anything in particular she said. It was more her presence. I had never been around a person who was as tender and gentle and good as Margaret Gaines. To be with her was to feel the presence of God Himself. And I've never gotten over it.

I know much more of Margaret's story now. She grew up in Pell City, and when she was nineteen, she felt that God was calling her to be a missionary in Tunisia. But she couldn't get any support because everybody said it was too dangerous for a pretty, single girl to go to North Africa on her own. But she went. Years later, she felt that God was calling her to the Palestinian village of Aboud. She never married, saying that she was married to Jesus, so it wouldn't be fair to a husband since her heart belonged to the Lord.

Margaret's life was greatly shaped by the hospitality and generosity of the Arab people, who received her as a gift to their community. In 1970, she established a church and a Christian elementary school that continues to this day, though in recent years serious heart ailments have forced Margaret back to her home town in Alabama. Currently, five Muslim villages surrounding Aboud send their children to the school. With few resources, Margaret developed the curriculum and created almost all of the visual aids herself. The Muslims who send their children to the school know full well they will be taught about Jesus as part of the educational program. A leading Muslim cleric in Aboud commented, "Sister Margaret shaped and changed the entire character of this village." A delegation of Muslim leaders told her on her last visit that they wanted to build a library in Aboud in her honor, as a monument to the love she brought there.

There are so many astounding stories from the life of my eighty-year-old spiritual grandmother. In 2006, I had the extraordinary privilege of going with her to Aboud. To see firsthand the places where she experienced remarkable miracles of biblical proportions has forever marked me. There were so many times she experienced supernatural provision from God while living among her people through multiple wars and astonishing oppression. One small story, out of countless examples, sums up for me the difference the Resurrection can make for a person living in a hostile world.

Sister Margaret was in the crowded village market one day when an angry man accosted her. Taking out his apparent frustration with Western military interference in the region, he began cursing her. He cursed the grave of her father, the grave of her mother, the grave of her grandparents, her God, and the God of her parents—everything he could think of. She felt the eyes of the entire village watching. As he hurled abuse at her, she quickly prayed for wisdom. When he was finally done, Margaret responded, "I am so sorry I hurt you. I never had any intention of hurting you. God loves you, and I love you. He loves this village and He wants to bless you. When you get over

being angry, will you remember I'm still your friend?"
Perplexed, he turned and walked away. In words that are
forever etched on my soul, Margaret said, "Satan doesn't
know how to respond to the gentleness of God's Spirit."

After this encounter, Margaret felt discouraged and
went back to her room to pray. "Oh God, what was the
meaning of this? Everybody in the village who could walk
was out on the streets today. What was this all about?" She
heard God say, "That was your pulpit. Those people will
never come to the church. But you preached My gospel
by demonstrating My Spirit."

Margaret recalls that there were many such situations
"that were unpleasant to the human heart. . . . But if we
can be God's person of peace in any given situation and a
witness—a living witness—to the unseen Lord . . . and live
out His Word and live out His teaching in everyday life as
He expects, then over time it makes a total difference."[4]
Margaret broke down in tears as she said, "Oh, if every
village had a living, breathing Spirit of Christ walking in its
midst, there would be a lot more peace. You are not going
to Palestine, perhaps. But you have this one little corner of
the world."[5] She taught us that when we run into human
cruelty and rage, "the sweetness of the Spirit will eventually
dissolve the acidity of the spirit that is coming against
you—and He will bring peace."[6]

It wasn't until much later that I began to understand
why I cry so much when I'm around Margaret. Even
though by the time I met her I had already started

following Jesus and was even stepping into ministry, there was something about her sense of peace, clarity, and simplicity that made me ache for a life I had not yet lived but seemed strangely familiar. Being around her helped me to understand that my name was not Legion. I didn't yet know what my true name was or what becoming human would really mean, but I knew I had a name as God's beloved son. I knew I had another identity. When you're living in a violent world full of zombies and you meet an authentic human being, you remember.

The most recent time that Sister Margaret stayed at our house, I got up very early one morning to find her staring out the back window into our yard. I will never forget the look I saw on her face. It was lit up with wonder as she watched the birds and squirrels and rabbits. It was a look of such awe and contentment. When she saw me, she began to talk about the simple things she was seeing in creation so far that morning and how beautiful it all was.

At eighty years old, Margaret still hears the music. Resurrection has made her a child of wonder, even now. I know now that this is what resurrection does to a person—it doesn't make you "religious," it makes you attentive to beauty on an unprecedented scale. Margaret has been to some difficult places and in some dark situations, but she doesn't see them the way that other people do. She sees "earth crammed with heaven,"[7] a world forever altered by resurrection.

What if people like us could become so intoxicated with

the beauty of God that we, like Margaret, could help other people begin to see "a world they'd like to live in"?

Walking the plank

People like Nellie Martin and Margaret Gaines have shown me a world I'd like to live in. I went through a short phase of needing to find proof that Jesus has risen from the dead, allegedly so I could convince somebody else, but probably more so I could convince myself. And if that kind of thing works for you, have at it, but it always left me cold. I could find a compellingly bright scholar to tell me why this all had to be true, only to find another compellingly bright scholar who could tell me why it couldn't be true, and go back and forth between books the rest of my life. I have yet to find a system so conclusive and airtight that I don't still have the option not to believe it. Ultimately, I don't know that I would do anything other than follow Jesus—simply because I have heard people's stories and seen things in the world that I cannot explain any other way unless God raised Jesus from the dead. That's all I've got. These days, I often remember my professor Stanley Hauerwas saying, "If you need a system to prop up your belief in Jesus of Nazareth, then worship your system."

Of course, there are many reasons to be cynical, and more than enough reasons to choose not to believe. Believing in a love that overcomes death is not soft and sentimental; it will always be the hard thing. Luckily, we aren't required to have perfect faith. There is more than enough room for hopeful doubters who, like Thomas, are drawn to reach out and grasp, to touch, rather than to just walk away. Perhaps the difference between "doubting Thomas" and a "cynical Thomas" is that Thomas doubted *in the direction of* Jesus rather than away from Him. That makes all the difference.

I remember a time in my life when I was wrestling with some issues, and Amanda and I went on vacation with her family, in the mountains of West Virginia. One day, after I had spent all morning reading my Bible in the woods, I was still struggling to trust what I sensed I was hearing from the Lord. While everyone else was still back at the house, I went down to the deserted pool, smelling the mountain air as I climbed up to the high diving board. As I stepped out toward the end of the board, anxiety rippled through my gut, and I realized there was another leap I had to make. I knew I would have to decide to plunge into trust, even though I didn't know exactly what it would mean for me. As I jumped, I let go of some things on my heart. Tasting the chlorine was a baptism of sorts.

I have had to take many such leaps since, though in all honesty, it often feels more like walking the plank than diving into a pool. No matter.

I don't know what it looks like for you right now, from where you're standing, to trust in the resurrected Jesus. I'm less concerned than ever before about the semantics of all of that. When I was growing up, we used to talk all the time about "inviting Jesus into your heart," which I did, kneeling by the coffee table in our den when I was five. The Jesus who was described to me was beautiful, so it was no wonder the prospect appealed to me so much then. I realize now that this shopworn phrase may actually be a little bizarre. Does Jesus shrink down like a character in a Disney movie and swim through your aorta?

I have a friend named Peter who pastors a church in South Africa. He's a remarkable man who, as a successful businessman, "asked Jesus to live in his heart" in 1973, after having what can only be described as a miraculous vision of Jesus while in a movie theater. He ended up on the front lines of the struggle between the faithful churches in South Africa and the tyranny of apartheid, and he struggled as a white South African for racial freedom at great risk. Now in his midsixties, he's an adventurous soul who loves to go to tribal groups who don't know anything about Jesus and figure out how to share the gospel in their language and imagery. A few years ago, he hiked for days to get to a tribal group of about twenty or so to share the love of Jesus with them. As he tried to explain to them the idea of "inviting Jesus into your heart," the translator looked puzzled.

"They don't have an equivalent word for *heart* here, Peter. For them, the seat of emotions is the liver."

A few minutes later, Peter led them all in a prayer to invite Jesus into their livers.

The point is that I don't think the language matters that much. You can invite Jesus into your heart or invite Him into your liver. Pick a vital organ, any vital organ, really. I've known too many people whose first encounter with resurrection life started with a feeble variation of "God, if You're really there, then . . ." to believe it matters what specific words we use. I do believe in resurrection and that all of this is real, but I don't believe it has a great deal to do with getting a doctrinal formulation just right or praying a magic prayer. We take our fears and our doubts and our dreams, and we toss them in the general direction of Jesus to do with as He sees fit. That's close enough.

7
sacraments

✧ ✧ ✧

The eucharistic celebration does not leave the world
unchanged. The future has occupied the present for a
moment at least, and that moment is henceforth an
ineradicable part of the experience of those who lived it.

GEOFFREY WAINWRIGHT,
EUCHARIST AND ESCHATOLOGY

Following Jesus turns out to be a full-contact sport. The bodily character of Christianity is perhaps its most defining feature. The scandal of Jesus of Nazareth, both in the first century and in the twenty-first, is that He is the Word made flesh. The Gnostic opponents both inside and outside the early Christian communities were perhaps the greatest threat to the new way of being human. Believing that matter was evil and only the spirit was good, they sought a form of higher enlightenment beyond the dank, smelly confines of the human body. Yet the message of Jesus was not bound up in taking flight from the human body, but in *restoring* it.

One of the chief reasons the Christians were persecuted in the early centuries was their peculiar insistence on the resurrection of the physical body. Exploring the catacombs in Rome a few years ago, I was struck by the extremes to which the early church went to bury the dead. Illegally, they snuck their corpses into underground caves in hopes of caring for them until the ultimate resurrection. Far from being morbid for these early Christians, these catacombs were symbols of hope, places for worship. Why go to such trouble if this were only some minor doctrinal quirk? Again, for the early church, the resurrection of Jesus from the dead as the uniquely begotten Son of God was by no means an isolated event. He was the prototype of the new humanity. What happened to Him would someday happen to them.

Of course many of those bodies would not be preserved—they would have been burned or would have decomposed—but if you can believe in something as radical as resurrection, overcoming the challenge of gathering bodies scattered by lions or burned to ashes shouldn't be too much of a leap for God. There are powerful implications in this for the people we love and the life that is to come. And we will get there soon enough.

But the centrality of the body for those who follow the resurrected Jesus isn't just about the life that is yet to come; it's about how we relate to other bodies *in the present*. Even before the Resurrection, we can already see the bodily, almost lusty character of the gospel. There is so much touching and tasting. We are often uncomfortable in our own skin and ill at ease in our bodies. But the gospel is a story about God in a body touching other bodies. So if you're going to get anything about Jesus, you can never graduate from the wonder of human touch. If life with God has any connection at all to Jesus, it's a bodily religion, and touch is the whole ball game. *Spirituality* is not a bad word for it, but the danger is always that we make it "something more" than the taste of brittle bread and sweet wine, the feel of wet flesh and calloused feet. For a religion that is all about bodies, then, it's not surprising that there is such an emphasis on bodily, physical practices. Bathing and blessing and eating are the primary colors of life with God. It is nothing more sophisticated (or less difficult to do) than that.

The God you can touch

Before Jesus came, it was not assumed that it would be possible to touch or be touched by deity. When God first showed Himself to Moses on Mount Sinai, His appearance was marked by thunder, flashes of lightning, the sound of a trumpet, and the mountain itself smoldering from the terror of it all.[1] From this early experience of the presence of God, the boundaries seem to be set. The people tell Moses, "You speak to us, and we will listen; but do not let God speak to us, or we will die" (Exodus 20:19). Throughout the rest of the Old Testament, the heartache is tangible— God wants to draw close to His people, but for whatever reason they, like us, are always finding different ways to keep their distance from Him.

The scandal of God in the flesh is that, in Jesus, we behold the God who can be *touched*. He is the God who had to eat and sleep and go to the bathroom. In Frederick Buechner's words, "Jesus is the Word made flesh, the truth narrated in bone and bowel, space and time. That is the story he is."[2] Yet the same apocalyptic terror, the same blinding holiness that was present on Mount Sinai is present on the Mount of Transfiguration, where Jesus for only a moment reveals to His disciples the same Sinai glory of the Exodus narrative. Once again, there is thunder and lightning and smoke. Once again, God's people cower in terror at the sight of it. But unlike the ancient story, that same Sinai presence reaches out and physically touches the disciples. "Don't be afraid," Jesus says.[3] In Moses' story, you might die simply by touching the mountain. When the sensuous God is fully revealed in Jesus Christ, you now touch not only the mountain, but the God who formed it.

The sheer volume of accounts documenting the touch of Jesus that healed the sick is striking. It was clearly not required for Jesus to touch anyone in order to make them well—John's Gospel makes it clear enough that Jesus has the same power of creative speech we read of in the opening lines of the Torah ("Let there be . . ."). What precisely is the practical function of touching blind men or lepers, if you only have to speak a word to heal them? There is something about Jesus that compels Him to human touch.

In the words of Stanley Hauerwas, "Lustily you love us, Mary-born Lord."[4]

A deaf man with a speech impediment is brought to Jesus. Characteristically, the man's friends beg Jesus to heal him. Little do they know that there is no need for an appeal. They don't know who they are dealing with. This earthy, sweaty Lord of dirt, this sensuous God-in-flesh never needs to be cajoled into touching other human beings. Taking the man away in private, where intimacy is safe and bodily care is appropriate, the Creator touches the creation. He is alternately tender and invasive: He puts His fingers into the man's ears. He spits. He touches the man's tongue. This is clearly not a scientific formula for healing. Looking up to heaven with human saliva on His fingertips, He lets out a sigh. "*Ephphatha*," He says. That is, "Be opened" (Mark 7:34). A mild germaphobe, I could probably become like Jack Nicholson's neurotic character in *As Good As It Gets* if I did not resist my tendencies. Jesus had no such squeamishness, either toward His own body or any other bodies.

A woman whose menstrual cycle has been a source of shame for twelve years comes to Jesus. The bleeding will not stop. In our allegedly enlightened modern world, we are squeamish enough about our own blood, let alone someone else's. The first time my wife asked me to go to the drugstore on that dreaded errand, I told her I would rather be caught buying crack in a back alley than bringing hygiene products to the front of the local CVS. How much

more so, given the prohibitions of Jewish law and the
Greek suspicion of the body, would this issue have been
a source of crippling shame for this woman? In this case,
the story doesn't highlight the divine compulsion of the
Creator to touch the creation seen in the ministry of Jesus;
it focuses on the woman's longing for human touch. So
convinced is she of the power of Jesus that she touches the
fabric of His robe. Touching coarse fabric that Jesus had
sweated in, dense with the odor of God Himself, would
be enough.

When the future reign of God comes breaking into our
present, there is more at stake than what we often call "spirituality." This movement of new humanity is not about a
detached, floating thing called a soul in a holding pen called
a body. This new way of being human is not an escapist fantasy for people who hope to leave planet Earth on some kind
of cosmic spaceship, like a sanctified Major Tom in David
Bowie's song "Space Oddity." This way of being human is
not for people who think their bodies are cages and want to
transcend the moment they are in. This way of being human
is not for people who don't like to dance or make love.

This is a protest against the body-defying, world-
denying principalities and powers that threaten to swallow
us up. This is resistance to religion that is less substantial
than the taste of crusty bread and sweet wine. It's in favor
of skin, in favor of laughter, in favor of music, in favor of
sweat. It's in favor of nakedness, but in protest to pornography. It's in favor of touch, but in protest to being

handled. It's in favor of the soul, but in protest to its dismemberment from the body.

It is as greasy as the touch of an oily finger on the T-zone of a teenager's face. It's as intrusive as the hands of a brother or a sister washing the dirt off your feet as you sit in awkward silence. It is as mysterious as the slow descent of a body into an ancient baptismal pool at midnight, with prayers and hymns offered up all around. It is as beautiful and disconcerting as the gore that flowed out of Jesus' side when it was torn by a spear, as spectacular as the lightning that flashed at Sinai, as plain and uneventful as a meal shared with a stranger.

It is high time we stopped sanitizing the scandal of a bodily gospel. Jesus' new way of being human is exceedingly good news for the legions around us who are in need of healthy touch. The salvation that has come to us from God's future is not "out there" or "up here." It is not the ascent of man into something higher, but the descent of God's Kingdom peace into the chaos of the present.

This may sound perfectly fine but entirely irrelevant to you. What good is it to know that touch played a profound role in the ministry of Jesus if He is no longer within touching distance? Yet that is why this forgotten scandal of new humanity, the bold but hidden true identity of the people of the future, is so significant. Jesus did not bring the comfort and delight of God's very own touch to humanity only to revoke it upon His ascension. It is why He sent the one He called "another Comforter,"

the Holy Spirit, to come and dwell within His new followers.[5] The same Spirit that rested on Him is now available to us—available to touch through us. The Spirit was
not given to make us private mystics. The Spirit wasn't
given to help us escape the world. The Spirit was given
to empower us to become God's touch for His creation,
right here and right now. Paul's language that we are the
body of Christ was not an elegant metaphor, but a state-
ment of fact. When we touch the splendid shambles
of the bodies around us, they receive a touch from Him.

Why the bodily gospel can become revolutionary again

We've looked at a lot of ways in which the world has
already changed, how the story of Legion is no longer one
random, bizarre account of a demon-possessed man in
first-century Palestine. It is seemingly now the story of all
of us. We are all beholden to a legion of voices and a forest
of screens. Interestingly, fewer and fewer of them are
human voices. The sound of human voices and the touch
of human skin is increasingly inefficient in our new world.
Sherry Turkle describes this phenomenon:

> We are changed as technology offers us substitutes for
> connecting with each other face-to-face. We are
> offered robots and a whole world of machine-
> mediated relationships on networked devices. As we

instant-message, e-mail, text, and Twitter, technology redraws the boundaries between intimacy and solitude. We talk of getting "rid" of our e-mails, as though these notes are so much excess baggage. Teenagers avoid making telephone calls, fearful that they "reveal too much." They would rather text than talk. Adults, too, choose keyboards over the human voice. It is more efficient, they say. Things that happen in "real time" take too much time. Tethered to technology, we are shaken when that world "unplugged" does not signify, does not satisfy. After an evening of avatar-to-avatar talk in a networked game, we feel, at one moment, in possession of a full social life and, in the next, curiously isolated, in tenuous complicity with strangers. We build a following on Facebook or MySpace and wonder to what degree our followers are friends. We recreate ourselves as online personae and give ourselves new bodies, homes, jobs, and romances. Yet, suddenly, in the half-light of virtual community, we may feel utterly alone. As we distribute ourselves, we may abandon ourselves. Sometimes people experience no sense of having communicated after hours of connection. And they report feelings of closeness when they are paying little attention. In all of this, there is a nagging question: Does virtual intimacy degrade our experience of the other kind and, indeed, of all encounters, of any kind?[6]

When Andre Gregory and Wallace Shawn were making their 1981 movie, *My Dinner with Andre*, which consists almost entirely of a dinner conversation between the two of them, they knew nothing of the world of social networking and nothing of the capacity we would have thirty years later to share so much more communication with so many more people. And yet Wally's critique now seems hauntingly prophetic: "I mean, we live in such ludicrous ignorance of each other. I mean, we usually don't know the things we'd like to know even about our supposedly closest friends!"[7]

As the world changes, all of our relationships have to be renegotiated, including our sexual relationships. In *Empire of Illusion: The End of Literacy and the Triumph of Spectacle*, Chris Hedges gives an unflinching account of the pornography industry and its broader effect on culture. As harsh and difficult as his account is to read, he successfully and entirely reframes the current conversation about sexuality in media. It is not a theological account; Hedges doesn't use the language of "sin." He makes the case not for pornographic sex being all "wrong," but provocatively suggests that "porn films are not about sex." Rather, Hedges claims,

> Sex is airbrushed and digitally washed out of the films. There is no acting because none of the women are permitted to have what amounts to a personality. The one emotion they are allowed to display is an unquenchable desire to satisfy men, especially if that

desire involves the women's physical and emotional
degradation. . . . Porn, which advertises itself as sex,
is a bizarre, bleached pantomime of sex. The acts
onscreen are beyond human endurance. The
scenarios are absurd. . . . Makeup and production
mask blemishes. There are no beads of sweat, no
wrinkle lines, no human imperfections. Sex is
reduced to a narrow spectrum of sterilized
dimensions. It does not include the dank smell of
human bodies, the thump of a pulse, taste, breath—
or tenderness. Those in the films are puppets,
packaged female commodities. They have no honest
emotions, are devoid of authentic human beauty,
and resemble plastic. Pornography does not promote
sex, if one defines sex as a shared act between two
partners. . . . Pornography is about getting yourself
off at someone else's expense.[8]

In a brilliant critique, Hedges compares the thousands of
pornographic images he and his wife subjected themselves
to in months of research attending porn conventions to the
images released that same year of prisoner abuse at Abu
Ghraib in Iraq. For Hedges, it was telling that the pictures
of naked Iraqi prisoners in forced erotic postures would
have been at home in the world of pornography.
Ultimately, our culture's private obsession with sexual violence cannot help but translate into other spheres of life.
For Hedges, pornography is symptomatic of a culture of

death. In the final analysis, "Porn is about reducing women to corpses. It is about necrophilia."[9]

How strange that in a culture so preoccupied with sexual images we have become a people so incapable of giving or receiving touch, giving or receiving affection. There was a time when the church was seen as an enemy of touch, the roadblock to genuine sexual expression. But in contrast to the pornographic empire run by the prince of the power of the air, the gospel of the firstborn of the dead can become scandalous once again. As it was in the first century, the image of the sensuous God at home in human skin can challenge a people who no longer know how to be at ease with their physical bodies.

Interestingly, *My Dinner with Andre* engages broad religious and ethical ideas without any pretense of being Christian in orientation. Andre sees the church, those following Jesus in His new way of being human in the world, as the potential resistance movement to the sophisticated technological age that keeps people apart instead of bringing us closer together. "We're talking about an underground, which did exist in a different way during the Dark Ages among the mystical orders of the Church. And the purpose of this underground is to find out how to preserve the light, life, the culture. How to keep things living."[10] The first time I heard that line, sitting on the couch in my den, I wept.

The future we find ourselves stumbling into is ideal for those who prefer to keep their adopted identity as Legion, for those who find peculiar comfort in an unending forest of a thousand competing voices. Given the inevitable messiness of authentic interactions with other people, it would be far less demanding if there were a route toward this new kind of humanity in which we were armed with nothing but a Bible or perhaps a laptop. Hermit-like, we would attempt to simply disconnect from the clatter of other human voices altogether, transcending the murkiness of community in search of the transcendent God. But resurrection has always been about bodies, and genuine community requires face-to-face, tangible connection.

This is the promise and problem of authentic Christianity—in Jesus, we aren't given a God who transcends the body. The early Christians understood that the only way they could know God was by getting around other people, other bodies, by getting closer to one another. Paul describes the church as "the body of Christ," of which Jesus, the prototype for the new way of being human, is the head. There is no way to be connected to the head, who is Jesus, without drawing close to bodies in community around us.

The church is Christ's bride. As Jesus made very clear to Peter, loving Him would not be an abstract exercise in existential religion or transcendental meditation. "If you love me, Peter—feed my sheep, take care of them" (John 21:17, my paraphrase). Even when Jesus was still with His disciples in His incarnate form, there was nothing otherworldly or overly mystical about how they related to each other. Jesus came to Peter to wash his feet one day, and Peter, humiliated that his Master would touch his feet, performing the service of a slave, protested, "It's not right for You to wash my feet." Jesus did not back off, nor did He affirm Peter's need for personal space. Rather He spoke harshly: "If you don't allow Me to do this, you have no part with Me" (John 13:6-8, my paraphrase).

For Jesus' earliest disciples and for us, growing closer to God has everything to do with growing closer to the community of actual embodied humans around us. There is no other path to being fully human in the way that Jesus was without relating as intimately with His friends as He did.

The power of touch

I've never seen the power of touch and blessing quite like I have in Marilynne Robinson's lovely novel *Gilead*. The tangible grace that passes from human hands through touch is present throughout the book, but my favorite demonstration comes early on, through baptism—though in this case, it isn't humans being baptized, but cats. An aging preacher named John Ames is writing his life's story for a son he knows he won't see grow up. He traces his calling to ministry back to when he baptized a litter of cats as a boy. "They were dusty little barn cats just steady on their legs, the kind of waifish creatures that live their anonymous lives keeping the mice down with no interest in humans at all, except to avoid them."[11] But finding the kittens sociable enough, one of the neighborhood girls swaddled it in a doll's dress, and they went forward with the baptismal rite. "I myself moistened their brows, repeating the full Trinitarian formula," Ames says.[12]

As Ames's own father was a minister, he eventually mustered the courage to ask him about it: "So finally I asked my father in the most offhand way imaginable what exactly would happen to a cat if one were to, say, baptize it. He replied that the Sacraments must always be treated and regarded with the greatest respect. That wasn't really an answer to my question. We did respect the Sacraments, but we thought the whole world of those cats."[13]

Looking back on his experience years later, he reflects,

I still remember how those warm little brows felt under the palm of my hand. Everyone has petted a cat, but to touch one like that, with the pure intention of blessing it, is a very different thing. It stays in the mind. For years we would wonder what, from a cosmic viewpoint, we had done to them. It still seems to me to be a real question. There is a reality in blessing, which I take baptism to be, primarily. It doesn't enhance sacredness, but it acknowledges it, and there is power in that. I have felt it pass through me, so to speak. The sensation is of really knowing a creature, I mean really feeling its mysterious life and your own mysterious life at the same time.[14]

Such is the intense physical power of one life conferring divine blessing on another. That's luckily not a privilege restricted to preachers.

Baptism

The story of the life, death, and resurrection of Jesus is only one story; but it's such a sweeping story that it's big enough to fit all of our little stories into it. All our laughter and heartbreaks, the dreams that died and the hopes that still live can somehow be mapped onto that one narrative. It's hard to say how one story can be expansive enough to accommodate so many others into it. I don't really know how it happens, but I do know *where* it happens—in the waters of baptism.

In the late second or early third century, the church understood how much was at stake in the descent into water. If you had attended a Christian gathering in those days, you might have come for months, or even years, listening to them sing hymns or share their teaching, before being allowed to participate in the mysterious Eucharistic meal at the center of their strange communal life. When it was time to partake of the bread and wine, you would be dismissed as an outsider. It wasn't until the community saw sufficient evidence that you really understood what you were getting yourself into that you would be allowed to participate in their baptismal rite.

After years of preparation, the moment would finally

come—perhaps at midnight on Easter. With the community chanting prayers and songs around you, you would be led into a pool or river where you would completely disrobe, descending naked into your watery grave. The officiant would ask you to affirm the basic doctrines of the church and renounce the devil and his works. This would culminate in an evocative, decisive moment, in which you would physically spit to the west, in the direction of Satan and his minions. Finally, you would be submerged into the waters of baptism and included in the full life of the church, able to partake of the sacred supper.

For generations, Christians have argued over exactly what occurs in the act of baptism and how it should be expressed. But for the early church, baptism was never understood as merely a ritualistic bath. There was something exotic and mystical about ceremonially participating in the death and resurrection of Christ, something that changed those who were baptized.

Though the early Christians believed that Jesus was the uniquely begotten Son of God, they did not believe His experience of resurrection was unique to Him. In language as mysterious as any ever conjured up in contemporary science fiction, they saw Jesus as the prototype for a new kind of human. His experience of rising from the dead was a foretaste of the life now available to all humanity. Thus Paul speaks of Jesus as "the beginning, the firstborn from the dead" (Colossians 1:18), and John's apocalypse also describes Him as "the firstborn of the dead" (Revelation 1:5). The baptismal rite told the story over and over of death and resurrection and a whole new species of humans who would share in this event.

I've baptized people in every conceivable body of water other than a Jacuzzi, and even that would not be out of the question. Early on at Renovatus, I baptized Blake on a Sunday night at a Baptist church kind enough to let us use their facility. I baptized her son Noah in a one-hundred-year-old elementary school auditorium. And I baptized her now-husband Jason in that old movie theater at Eastland Mall. All very different locations, but always the same reality—their stories submerged into that age-old story of death and resurrection.

Last year at Renovatus, we had our first midnight baptism service. We started at 11:30 on Saturday night, and when the clock struck midnight on Easter Sunday morning, I took my position behind the baptismal pool. The setting of those early baptisms somehow feels more exotic in my mind than ours today. Our baptismal pool is an odd little borrowed contraption that, depending on how you look at it, is actually kind of a hot tub on wheels with a cross on it. As the candidates started making their way to the pool that night, though, amid the dancing shadows of dim candlelight, I was struck by how much the rectangular box looked like a coffin. Hot tub or no, there was nothing remotely normal about what we were about to do.

Like John the Baptist, I felt a faint trembling in my hands. I wasn't about to handle the body of the only begotten Son of God, but this was close enough. I was about to handle the bodies of sons and daughters, no less, who just like Jesus will one day be swallowed up in resurrection. How could I not quiver? I was overcome by the knowledge that these bodies, this wet flesh I was holding with the same hands I use to take out the trash or carry in the groceries, would one day be raised from the dead. Not detached, floating spirits but these very bodies will live forever in the presence of Christ and the angels. Sometimes, it is more than I can take. How does one properly handle such bodies? How can I adequately value such a thing? I am fairly certain I still don't understand any of this. And if I did? I'm afraid I might tremble during a simple handshake.

Touching feet and touching the future

Jesus gave many bodily practices to this new human community that would bring God's future crashing into the present whenever we engaged them. We just don't like to do some of them much. Foot washing is one of the most primary of these futuristic practices. In a world where being served and being first are the very definition of power, this one tiny act inverts the natural order of the universe. For those few moments, everything we've learned about success comes under Christ's final judgment. This gives us a glimpse into the radical inversion of power that will come when Jesus runs things.

Foot washing is perhaps the most futuristic practice of

the church, though not many people really believe that.
Most Christians think they are being cutting edge and
futuristic when they have busy graphic presentations running on a Mac during their worship times. Removing our
shoes before one another is a jarring practice even for
church people—it's like listening to a Radiohead album in
the 1950s. But precisely because it is so jarring, so unnatu-
ral, so unlike the empire of illusion created by the prince
of the power of the air, it is undeniably powerful. I don't
know if we've ever had a more potent experience at
Renovatus than we had washing one another's feet on a
Sunday morning. It's a page right out of the church
growth manuals, really.

Despite my native germaphobia, I would wash anybody's feet and I'd drink after anyone in a common cup
Communion, such is my confidence in the sacredness of
the moment. When we engage in these practices, I don't
just *hope* that God shows up. His presence is guaranteed
when we do these things. That said, I am considerably
more squeamish about having my own feet washed. To put
it nicely, my feet are not my best feature. I understand why
Peter protested when Jesus wanted to wash his feet. I don't
know anybody as holy as Jesus, but I have yet to meet a
person who I felt wasn't far above washing my feet. When
I feel the touch of human hands on my hairy toes and calloused soles, it is terrible in all the ways it must be for
Christ Himself to touch my most unlovely places with His
tenderness. Every time, the tears burn my eyes. And as my

self-consciousness and self-confidence begin to crumble, it's not just my feet that are being washed; it's the love of God like a warm balm on a bruised and battered soul.

The practice of anointing the sick with oil is another futuristic rite we are given: "Are any among you sick? They should call for the elders of the church and have them pray over them, anointing them with oil in the name of the Lord. The prayer of faith will save the sick, and the Lord will raise them up; and anyone who has committed sins will be forgiven" (James 5:14-15).

What does this have to do with the future? Remember, the gospel of the new humanity is not that there will be a resurrection of the spirit, but that there will be a resurrection of the body. The same thing that happened to Jesus in His bodily resurrection will one day happen to us. When we anoint the sick and pray for them, we are anticipating the day when Christ will heal all of our broken bodies, transforming us into His own likeness. Not only are we *anticipating*, we are mysteriously *participating*. In the words of Herbert McCabe, we should view "the sacrament of anointing the sick as an exploration of the meaning of the bodily care men have for each other, and see its ultimate meaning in Christ's care for our bodies culminating in the resurrection itself."[15]

Early in our time at Renovatus, Sally Tolentino and her husband, Pedro, led several of us on a mission trip to Mexico to help a local church put together a series of open-air evangelistic services. They asked me to be the evening speaker. On the day of the event, I saw the signs and banners all over town. Unable to read Spanish, I asked Pedro what the signs said.

"Come expecting a miracle," he said.

Oh, boy. Immediately my heart sank. I have no doubt whatsoever about God's capacity to heal broken bodies in the same way that Jesus did in the Gospels. But I had no direct experience of that myself.

Sure enough, people took the sign at face value. When I got done preaching, the crowds began lining up, and I prayed with people deep into the night—much longer than the sermons I preached. One by one, they came with stories of profound brokenness and deep needs for healing. What was I to offer them? I cannot say who did or did not get healed, and by no means (then or now) did I feel that I was some great healing evangelist come to save the nation. But I did experience a deep inward transformation that week. As I prayed for these people, I was overcome by the knowledge that they were expecting me to touch them on God's behalf. Whether or not I was prepared for such a mission was irrelevant—that is what they had come for, and touch them on God's behalf was what I had to do. Without thinking about it, I found myself touching each person differently. With some, I held their hands. Others, I embraced. With yet another set, I laid my hands gently on their heads. I stooped to hold others.

Unsure of what was happening to them, I knew what was happening to me—I was being caught up in God's heart for His sons and daughters. That I was overwhelmed, ordinary, and decidedly not a faith healer didn't matter. I wasn't like one of the televangelists who seem to have come from another planet. But I was nonetheless sent from the future. There is nothing more futuristic than laying hands on another body in Jesus' name, because it anticipates the healing that is yet to come for the entire creation. Healing evangelist or not, this feels like science fiction now. In my head, I hear David Bowie singing, "This is Major Tom to Ground Control, I'm stepping through the door . . ."[16]

Communion

We aren't just touching the future. We are tasting it. It always comes back to the meal. Like the disciples on the road to Emmaus, no matter how clueless and blind we might be, when we break the bread, all of a sudden we can see Jesus again. It's always the meal. Like being in Sister Margaret's kitchen in Pell City, Alabama, or savoring my grandmother's corn bread with a glass of Tang, it's the taste of the meal that always brings me home. So much of being at home with God has to do with coming back to the meal in which He offers us the body and blood of Jesus, His Son.

When we come to the table, there is nothing worse than feeling that we don't belong there. When I was in late middle school and early high school, I went through an unfortunate fashion phase. I kept trying to dress like my favorite R & B groups: I wore shirts and ties with shorts like Boyz II Men; the next year, I wore a long black coat with a hoodie and a silk shirt, like the guys in Jodeci. For an acne-ridden, gangly white kid, this was not a recipe for acceptance. I remember walking through the cafeteria with my lunch tray, looking for a place to sit—outwardly non-chalant, but inside scared to death that nobody would make room for me at their table.

At church, my fear was not that I wasn't cool enough, but that I wasn't holy enough. I was never excited about that meal. Fearing judgment as I did, the only Scripture I thought about with regard to Communion was 1 Corinthians 11:29, the passage in which Paul warns, "He that eateth and drinketh unworthily, eateth and drinketh damnation to himself, not discerning the Lord's body," as the King James Version puts it.

In our church when I was a boy, we understood the Lord's Supper to be only symbolic, so there didn't seem to be a lot to gain from a ceremonial reenactment. On the other hand, eat and drink unworthily—and you *die*. I thought of receiving the elements as a form of Russian roulette. If you were holy enough, nothing bad would happen. But if there was a bullet in the chamber . . . well, then you'd know for sure you weren't holy!

I remember hearing a pastor say, based on that passage, that he thought someone in his congregation had died because there was unconfessed sin in their life. So when I got the little cup of juice (as we did in those days), I wished

I could casually dump it over my shoulder while everybody else drank. That way, nobody in the church would think I was a filthy sinner for not taking Communion *and* I wouldn't be struck dead for partaking unworthily. It seemed like a reasonable compromise.

This fear seems odd to me now. After all, the primary scandal of Jesus' earthly ministry was that He shared table fellowship with the wrong people: "Why does your teacher eat with tax collectors and sinners?" (Matthew 9:11). It was the practice for which Jesus was most vilified in His religious community. The Pharisees knew that to share a meal eyeball-to-eyeball with another human being was to validate that person.

In Luke's account of the first Communion, when the Passover meal is first transformed, even Judas is invited to participate, although He is about to betray Jesus. And Peter is invited to participate, though He is about to deny Jesus.

When Jesus offered up His own body and blood for the world, He spread a table for the outcast and the broken. We come to the table not because we are holy, but because we are in need of His holiness. We come to the table not because we are strong, but because we are weak and in need of His strength.

Today, I have a much higher view of this sacrament than I did when I was young, yet I am no longer afraid of it. Though I don't share the Catholic view of transubstantiation per se, I agree with many of the Reformers who understood that something of the real presence of Christ is available in the meal—in ways too mysterious for us to explain, but present nonetheless.

God is visibly present in the world in two principal ways: through the people of God and through this meal; both are manifestations of the body of Christ. Yet here is the irony: If the scandal of Jesus was that He was always touching the wrong people and inviting the wrong people to the table—how on earth can we think the Communion meal now is for the extra holy or the super spiritual? To say we need to be completely cleaned up before Communion is like saying we need to get well so we can take our medication.

Though it is true that the apostle Paul gives a strong warning about Communion, the context is very particular. Apparently, there were some in Corinth who, mirroring the broader practice of their culture, had the meal around the table with the rich and elite within their Christian community, while those with lesser status were left to eat whatever leftovers remained.[17] It was the opposite of how Jesus practiced table fellowship. They were taking the meal meant for the ordinary and making it for the elite, taking the table spread for the broken and offering it only to the whole. And in this way, they were dividing the body of Christ in a sick parody of what this act was meant to be. No wonder Paul speaks so harshly of this practice!

But by no means does this mean that now only the super spiritual can come to the table. We come to the table not because we have power, but because there is power available to us. We don't come perfect, we come humbly, hungry and thirsty for righteousness; we come desperate for God. Shame should not keep us from touching Jesus through this meal any more than shame kept the broken from touching Jesus in His incarnate body.

We come to the table every week at Renovatus. And as we do, we understand it to be a table for the broken. Every week, I read the words of this simple Communion invitation just before we are served:

> This is the table, not of the church, but of the Lord. It is made ready for those who love Him and for those who want to love Him more. So come, you who have much faith and you who have little; you who have been here often and you who have not been here long; you who have tried to follow and you who have failed. Come, because it is the Lord who invites you. It is His will that those who want Him should meet Him here.[18]

We may come broken, but we also come whole. Because when we take Communion, we taste the future. In ways similar to my bicycle when I was a kid, the table has become a time machine for me. It draws me back to the meal Jesus ate with His disciples before He was crucified. It draws me back to the cross where His mangled body hung limp. It transports me to the future, to the table where we will gather with Christ after the resurrection of our bodies.

My wife, Amanda, wrote a lovely hymn that we sing whenever we take Communion at Renovatus. It goes like this:

Sacramental love, borne of fruit and grain,
Act of ages past, this we do again.
Shadow of the feast, that is and has not been,
We crucify ourselves, that we may call you kin.

This mouth shall taste, these lips will sing
Of all our loss to gain a King,
Our fellowship forged in the flood,
We eat your flesh, we drink your blood.

When I would partake of practices like these, I used to hope that God would show up. I'm not hoping anymore—I know He is present when we gather for Communion, baptize, wash each other's feet, and lay hands on people in prayer. That's why we handle these practices—or more precisely, each other—with great reverence. We are touching the future, and that is a combustible thing.

Invasion

Everything about these bodily practices is odd—from Communion to anointing people with oil to baptism. It is odd whether we do it at midnight or at eleven o'clock on a Sunday morning, odd in a river or in a movie theater. It is odd to place our entire life stories into the life and story of a Man we've never met in the flesh. It is odd that something as basic as bathing can become itself a narrative of death and resurrection. When people get baptized and begin finding meaning through the strange new meal of Communion, they openly take ownership of the oddness of what God is doing in the world today through Jesus of Nazareth and the assorted misfits and dreamers who call Him Lord. It is a decisive step we don't easily come back from.

It's no wonder that when we begin, in whatever small measure, to step into God's future by living in the story of the resurrected Christ, others don't know what to do with us. These new practices help us develop some of the characteristics of Jesus, the prototype of our new humanity, the one whom the apostle Paul provocatively called "the last Adam,"[19] and it challenges the world around us.

Being around a new human can be frightening at first. Like the reaction to the man with the legion of demons who found himself sitting calmly at the feet of Jesus, people may see our newfound orientation as a judgment on their disorientation; they may see our newfound peace as a judgment on their chaos. Paul describes this transformation into new life with no less restrained speech than Matthew's apocalyptic description of Jesus' resurrection:

You He made alive, who were dead in trespasses and sins, in which you once walked according to the course of this world, according to the prince of the

power of the air, the spirit who now works in the
sons of disobedience, among whom also we all once
conducted ourselves in the lusts of our flesh,
fulfilling the desires of the flesh and of the mind.
(Ephesians 2:1-3, NKJV)

Once dead, but now alive—following the firstborn of the
dead, our prototype.

Paul's description of our existence before resurrection is
that of being dead in trespasses and sins. Predating our
contemporary horror-film images, it is surely a fascinating
portrait of our notion of the "walking dead."

For me, there will never be a computer-generated zombie
apocalypse to compete with the 1978 atmospheric chiller,
Invasion of the Body Snatchers. An exercise in restrained creepi-
ness, the film stars Donald Sutherland, Brooke Adams,
Veronica Cartwright, a very young-looking Jeff Goldblum,
and Leonard Nimoy in a notable non-Spock role. As alien
beings slowly begin to clone people, hatching their new
identical-looking counterparts from mysterious pods, the
world is repopulated. The small band of humans who have
thus far resisted the process learn how to walk among these
walking dead, mimicking their slow, shuffling movements
and empty stares.

Toward the end of the film, Sutherland and Cartwright
have been separated, and she continues to perpetuate her
act as a fully functional human in a world of soulless
beings. Finally, she stumbles upon Sutherland's character

again, and expresses her joy to see a human companion. In the delightfully eerie closing scene, though, we see that he, too, has joined the ranks of the undead. Instead of embracing his old friend, he points at her and lets out a primal, otherworldly howl, letting the rest of the pod people know he has spotted an authentic human being. Without further commentary or resolution, the credits roll.

These days, people who claim to be followers of Jesus may be "scary" in all the wrong ways. They may act in the same kind of aimless panic, fear, and accusation as the rest of the world. But what if these people instead began to experience the power of resurrection in such a way that they, like the man who once had the legion of demons, were distinguishable precisely because they were so authentically human in such an increasingly inhuman world? What if, in a world full of fear and violence, their lives were marked by such joy and peace and perspective—the unalterable confidence of those who believe resurrection has already changed the world—that they began to scare the natives?

We are no longer living in a time when anything inhuman would scare us. We aren't frightened by vampires or werewolves or zombies—in fact, we market teenage romances about falling in love with them! In a world where anger and blame and rage and condemnation are considered normal, where technology and machines continue to replace authentic relationships, there is nothing nearly as frightening as an authentic human being. In a world where corporations are brainwashing everybody to think the same way and want the same things out of life, being fully alive and fully human is scary indeed.

No wonder the early Christians practiced baptism in such radical, decisive terms. The day would inevitably come when the truth of their authentic human experience would be exposed in a hostile environment. Given such an unpleasant prospect, it is better to disrobe early in the journey and take the plunge. There would be no going back. It turns out that removing their skivvies to be baptized naked might actually be the least radical thing about such people.

8
community

✧ ✧ ✧

In the busy, teeming crowd, which as community is
both too much and too little, man becomes weary of
society, but the cure is not in making the discovery that
God's thought was incorrect. No, the cure is precisely to
learn all over again the most important thing, to
understand oneself in one's longing for community.
SØREN KIERKEGAARD, *WORKS OF LOVE*

The churches I grew up in practiced all of the sacraments I
mentioned earlier—baptism, Communion, foot washing,
laying hands on the sick and anointing them with oil. But
there was a wilder side to our liturgy as well. The physical-
ity of corporate worship wasn't just in the eating and bathing and blessing, it was also in dancing and shouting.
Christian communities are always built around the sacraments, but they are also built on the shared kinetic joy we
experience in worship together.

Our prayers and worship were full-bodied and hot-
blooded. I grew up going to camp meetings where the altar

calls could go on for three hours after the sermon was done. People spoke in tongues, shouted, danced, wept, ran, and knelt—sometimes, it seemed, simultaneously. I remember being a little afraid of all of that when I was a small boy, and perhaps in a way I still am. Was it the noise I feared, or the reverent terror I felt of the Mount Sinai God? Or was I afraid of the joy itself? For whatever else we might have been uptight about, you could not have found a happier bunch of folks. Ecstatic with God, people leapt and rejoiced and prayed deep into the night. These were people I loved and respected, people who I knew knew God. Many of them knew what it was to have lived hard and to have worked with their hands, but their response to God and to one another was exquisitely tender. How badly I wanted to join them, to feel what they were feeling, to experience what they were experiencing.

They are in me and I am in them, and there is a part of me that will always feel at home in those settings. There is also a part of me that may always feel like an outsider. I wanted to be on the inside of all of that, which is why I went forward at every altar call. (I was trying to stay ready for the Rapture, I guess.) I craved the electricity they felt; I wanted my blood to run hot with God too. Whatever they had tapped into, I wanted it.

Instead, self-conscious and obsessed with my own unworthiness to encounter a God who sparkled like that, afraid that the fire that kept them warm might incinerate me, I drew close but always felt distant. It was as if the

entire room was in on something that I didn't get. Unable
to enter into their joy, I nonetheless gathered around the
fire. Always pensive, my eyes were squeezed tightly shut
and my head stayed bowed down. The old-time prayer war-
riors would get in my ear and shout instructions to let go,
to loosen up, to get me shouting. It was an abandonment I
wanted, but it didn't seem accessible to me. It was all I
knew and all I wanted to know, and yet I couldn't seem to
make it into the center of the circle.

And what was I so pensive about? Everything from the
end of the world to the blasphemy of the Holy Ghost, the
one sin Jesus said couldn't be forgiven. I made fun of one of
the healing preachers and imitated him. I thought I might
go to hell for that. I took Communion the week after I had
a sexual dream. Probably took damnation onto myself.
I was always certain I had breached the salvation contract.

When the big-time evangelists laid hands on people, we
knew God was with them because the people "fell out under
the power." They were overcome with God, intoxicated with
the Spirit. I wanted to get lost in it like they did. I wanted a
power that ran through my veins and crackled underneath
my skin; I wanted to wake up at the feet of Jesus or wherever
it is you go when you are under the power of the Holy
Ghost. Service after service, I came forward for prayer, waiting for the preacher to touch me. The altar looked like a
Civil War battlefield, with bodies strewn all about of those
"electrocuted" with God. And every time, it was the same
result: I was the last man standing, bobbing along on the

surface of the ocean while everyone else was submerged in the waves. And I wondered what was wrong with me.

Then there was a particular night at the Lincolnton Church of God when I was fourteen. This was the church my dad had served until I was two, just a good rural Pentecostal church. During my teenage years, my dad was president of East Coast Bible College, and he went out preaching on the weekends to raise money for the school. The East Coast Chorale, a choir made up of students, would sing and he would preach. I was excited that we were going to Lincolnton that Sunday night, because I was convinced it was home to the prettiest girls in the Church of God. Sweet tea–drinking Southern girls with the Holy Ghost, and one was even a cheerleader. That week my parents had bought me a new sport coat at the Gap. When I wore it to church, it was not the power of the Holy Ghost I most wanted to experience.

From early in the evening, there was something different about that night, something magical. In Pentecostal terms, "God showed up." There was something uninhibited about the worship as the choir sang that night, and when my dad got up to preach, even he seemed to speak with more authority than usual. And the people kept right on rejoicing. It was like a brilliant improvisational jazz performance between the preacher, the Word, and the people, one of those times when you don't know exactly where you're going, but you know it's going to be good, and you know you're going there together, so you trust each other.

We would have said that the glory of God was falling in that room.

When the choir got up to sing some more, the place came unglued. There was such a purity about the joy we felt, as if the entire building could go up in smoke. Years later, a bolt of lightning struck the steeple of that building and it burned down. I wasn't surprised, because I had seen lightning strike it once before—the lightning of God's presence on Mount Sinai in all its splendor.

Typically, when I would sing, I never sang like I wanted to because I didn't feel worthy to worship a God who seemed made of pure electricity. But that night, for the first time, something was different. It wasn't about the song I was singing, but the song that was being sung over me. We sang in church for hours every week, but that night I heard the music in a new way. And the Spirit of the music drew me in.

I felt the delight of God over me and the freedom of God within me. It wasn't just adrenaline, but a sense of my own belovedness. And for the first time, I felt myself being caught up. Singing and rejoicing midway down a long pew on the far left side of the church, I felt so much joy that I thought I would die if I didn't leap. So I began to move back and forth on my tiptoes, like an aerobic exercise from a 1980s Richard Simmons video. And then I started jumping. Before I knew it, I felt as if jumping was not enough—I had to dance!

Self-conscious, unworthy, and ever mindful of the

sweet tea–drinking girls—remember, I was fourteen—I
had plenty of reasons to exercise restraint. But the joy was
too overwhelming. Reluctantly, I felt myself giving in.
That night it felt like the music, and whatever was behind
it, took me over. I gave in just a little, and it was as if I
had magic shoes. My feet began to move in an unchoreo-
graphed primal joy, and the rest of me went along for
the ride.

Moments later, even dancing did not seem quite
enough. I ached to leave the safe confines of the pew, to
dance without the constraints of the cushioned pew behind
me and the wooden rail in front. But I couldn't do that.
I did not want to be a spectacle. Even though I was caught
up with God, there was just enough "cool" left in me to
bristle at the thought of standing out and drawing attention to myself. I had given in to the leaping and the jumping, but I drew the line at dancing in the aisle.

There were about three hundred people in the room
that night. While I was locked in this inner tug-of-war
between my pride and the music, the strangest thing happened. A guy singing in the choir on the back riser jumped
down to the floor and walked over to the pew where I was
sitting. He stepped past the people standing to the left of
me, grabbed my left arm, which was raised in worship, and
physically led me out of the pew and into the aisle.

The moment my feet hit the aisle, I took off. I danced
my way all the way down the left side of the church.
I danced my way through the door into the lobby. I danced

through the lobby to the other side of the church, and
danced up the right-hand aisle until I got to the front. Then
I danced back and forth across the front of the church.
I danced and danced until I could not dance anymore.

I have not had an experience quite like that before or
since. For the record, this is not a story about the value or
lack thereof of liturgical dancing. I do not know precisely
how to account for everything I felt and experienced that
night, much less how you might account for it. I only
know that it was the night I first heard the music, the night
I let the music carry me beyond myself. There were a few
hours during which I was completely oblivious to girls and
self-loathing and overanalysis. Have I lived that purely for
many hours of my life since then? I can't say.

I believe that somewhere, somehow, you've heard the
music. Distant or close, you've heard the song of your
belovedness. It's a song of unrestrained joy, a song of hope
and belonging. A song that calls you into the future. Can
you even imagine what it would be like to dance the dance
of children, the dance before innocence was lost? To dance
with the abandon of a boy on a bike or a girl on a trampoline, lost in wonder, lost in the knowledge that you are loved,
unaware of what anyone else will say or think?

There are so many reasons to stay in the pew. The
Spirit, after all, is a disruptive force, and who can say
where the dance will take you? I understand why you may
not trust the music. We're all older now and we have
responsibilities. But what if the dance is what you were

born for? To be uninhibited and unrestrained before your Creator, to be unfettered by the foreign identity and expectations that have been assigned to you?

I'm not the preacher here; this is after hours. I only want you to trust the music, to trust the song of your belovedness, and to trust the Spirit who sings it over you. I do not want to be intrusive. I don't want to coerce you into anything. Don't you see that the dance has always been in you and that somebody put it there on purpose? Whether or not you give in to the dance is up to you.

Dancing, even dancing in the Spirit, often requires that somebody come down out of the choir, take us by the hand, and lead us into the aisle. No matter how much we might hear and feel the summons to dance, we are also made for community. And if we are going to follow the music all the way through into our identity as the beloved and all the way back to the source of the music, it will take some brothers and sisters to lead us there. Like the lame man whose friends carried him on a mat to Jesus, cut a hole in the roof, and lowered him down, we need people who will pick us up and carry us into the presence of God. We need people who recognize the music within us, and who love us enough to pull us into the place of freedom.

What real community looks like

Since we started Renovatus, I've seen this story enacted over and over again. I've seen sons and daughters, already

beloved of God and sung over by the Spirit, finally begin to
dance—all because somebody loved them enough to take
them by the hand and lead them out into the aisle. I've
seen people move from addiction and inhibition and
restraint into finally dancing the dance of their belovedness, finally giving in to the song that God was singing
over them all along.

One of those people is my friend Dianne. She was
Dennis and Elizabeth Donahue's neighbor. When they first
got to know Dianne, she looked ill and old, though she was
only fifty at the time. Dianne was estranged from her family, as her children had been taken away years before by the
Department of Social Services. She was in a relationship
with a live-in boyfriend who abused her physically and
emotionally, as did his extended family. At times, she had
been taken to a place near West Jefferson, North Carolina,
and virtually held captive for months with no way of
returning to Charlotte. She had been hospitalized at one
point for the stress this caused.

Dianne lived in squalor in government-subsidized housing. The house had no heat or electricity, and at times no
water. She had a poor relationship with her landlady.
Dianne had no money, insurance, or food stamps. She was
often disoriented, depressed, and paranoid. Overweight
and living with constant abuse, she had no self-confidence.
When Elizabeth began to visit with her, she sought to gain
Dianne's trust and that of her paranoid, bipolar significant
other. When she asked Dianne if she'd like to attend our

church, she jumped at the chance. Over time, she began attending a community life group led by my wife, Amanda.

As the Donahues gained her trust, things began to turn around for Dianne. Elizabeth developed a relationship with the landlady and began to serve as an advocate. She worked with the Social Security Administration to procure income, Medicaid, and food stamps for Dianne. A visit to a primary care physician was arranged so that Dianne could receive treatment for a host of health issues. When she had gall bladder surgery, Elizabeth stayed through the night with her. She later arranged for Dianne to get glasses and hearing aids. Monthly appointments were set with a psychiatrist and psychologist to help ease Dianne's emotional anguish. And she was encouraged through significant weight loss to avoid adult-onset diabetes.

Her new friends at Renovatus bought her clothes and undergarments. She received a computer and printer, and was given lessons to learn how to use them. They even took her to visit her dad's and stepmom's graves.

People started including her in their holiday celebrations, and when Dianne turned fifty-five, they threw a surprise birthday party for her that nearly twenty of her new friends from Renovatus attended. Ultimately, she was encouraged to reestablish her relationship with her family as well, and now her sister, brother, stepfather, and daughter are all back in her life.

On a regular basis, Lauren, a woman in our congregation, monitors and distributes Dianne's medications.

A monthly activity calendar is kept to arrange rides for her to and from our worship services and transportation to and from grocery shopping, and a group from Renovatus meets with her in her home every week for Bible study. With their prompting, Dianne has become more independent, purchasing bus passes and feeling comfortable traveling on her own, as well. There are little things, too, that have helped Dianne understand her identity as a beloved daughter of God—she is treated to salon visits and pedicures on occasion.

Dianne's newfound dance was not good news for everybody from her former life, however. In the story of the man with the legion of demons, we've seen how these powers become threatened when people begin to live in their freedom. When they receive the song of their belovedness and their identity as daughters and sons, those around them who aren't yet dancing are afraid of what's happening to them. There will always be people who will be threatened by your dance and intimidated by your freedom.

Dianne has come to trust her new friends so much that Elizabeth, Blake, and Lauren now have durable power of attorney, as well as living will and health care power of attorney for her. Elizabeth and Dennis ultimately were able to get Dianne out of her terrible living conditions. They put all her things in storage, cleaned her house, and turned it back to the landlady. They moved Dianne into an extended stay hotel for three months while they sought new accommodations through the Charlotte Housing

Authority. With the help of another friend at Renovatus, they located a condo for Dianne across the street from my house. That led to a confrontation in which the Donahues had to explain to Dianne's abusive boyfriend (whom she calls The Rat) that he could not live in her new home. That conversation didn't go very well.

One Saturday morning, I heard horrible screaming coming from the front yard. I thought at first Amanda must be watching a movie, but when I opened my front door, I saw Dennis and Elizabeth in a tense confrontation with a man and woman in our driveway.

Dennis is one of the gentler people I know, admired for his jovial demeanor and disarming wit, so he was the last person I would have expected to see in a heated showdown. The last person, that is, except for Elizabeth, who spent years as the public relations director at SeaWorld and is the picture of cordiality and restraint.

That day, The Rat and his mother (a character I honestly think I saw in an old episode of *The X-Files* years ago) had followed Dennis and Elizabeth from Dianne's former home until they got them to pull over in front of my house. As I stepped out onto the porch, I heard The Rat hurling every filthy epithet imaginable at Dennis and Elizabeth. As he directed crude, sexually explicit insults at Elizabeth, I saw Dennis (who, like me, is about six foot five) about to lose his cool. In a moment of fury, he actually threw down his glasses and started to walk past me, saying, "I don't care if you are here, Pastor . . ." I simply put my hand on his chest and said, "We aren't going to do that, Dennis." Though every impulse in him was screaming to fight for his wife's honor, he didn't resort to violence. After some calming words from me (and some even raunchier responses from The Rat), the duo finally sped off, with The Rat shouting all the while, "I know where you live, Donahue . . . and I'll be back!"

The Donahues were shaken by the experience. They weren't looking for a fight, but Dianne was their friend and they loved her. And if taking care of her meant stepping between the abused and the abuser, so be it.

This is what is so messy and so beautiful about Christian community. What separates authentic followers of Jesus from so many others in the world is a relentless tenderness toward human bodies. We consider the care for all earthly bodies to be directly under our jurisdiction, because we believe God inhabited a human body, making sacred our human anatomy. God tabernacled in flesh, then decreed that our very bodies would be the temple of the Holy Spirit. It is why Christians, while we need not be squeamish, must in turn be protective of fragile bodies. The body of a screaming baby and the body of an incontinent senior citizen, even a body locked away in prison. A body in inner-city Detroit and a body in Afghanistan. It is the birthright of the church to show the world what it means to cherish, value, and care for human bodies on an unprecedented level, because we believe both that human beings are made in the image of God and that God touched the ground in human form. We know holiness when we see it because the most holy people touch and regard other bodies with the greatest tenderness. As I have seen in Dianne's story, leading people into the dance of freedom is messy business—but it is more than worth it.

I often tell people I wasn't sure if I was a Christian before we started Renovatus—to which they laugh nervously (especially if they are part of our church). But even as a lifelong product of the church, I have never experienced the level of vulnerability or the depth of relationship anywhere else in my life that I have here. I feel like the guy from the old Hair Club for Men commercials: "I'm not just the president . . . I'm also a client." I'm not just the pastor, I'm a body under renovation. Because if God is saving anybody at Renovatus, He's saving me, and I have plenty to be saved from and even more to be saved *to*.

To be clear, I don't find any of this remotely easy. I'm an only child, and though I learned how to get along with people and relate to them by virtue of the rough-and-tumble realities of growing up in a preacher's home—you're thrown into all sorts of environments with all sorts of people and only the strong survive—I'm happier to be on my own most of the time. I had never experienced the kind of community I've found at Renovatus, so how in the world am I supposed to lead it? It's very humbling when you realize you need the very people you set out to "save" to save you. I wish this were merely a rhetorical device, but it is more true than I'd like to admit. And because I take seriously the idea that Jesus is made known to us through the actual bodies of His people, I do not think it sacrilegious to say that God is saving me through them. We are no more impressive than our Teacher, the suffering servant of Isaiah 53, mocked and scarred. But resurrection has made our scars a source of hope and healing as we open up our broken lives to the world.

When we started Renovatus, I didn't claim to know a whole lot about what God was saying to us. But I did know this: He would form our congregation around the gifts and the callings of the people He was going to send to us. That is very counterintuitive. The best way strategically to build anything, let alone a church, is with a strong central vision that everyone can rally around. But when your vision is for "liars, dreamers, and misfits" to come in, and you have the sense that they are all coming in with something we need, it's more beautiful and much more tedious. In the world we live in, it requires a patience that is both exotic and exhausting.

It is hard to summarize how we do what we do, especially since our goal has always been to embed this way of living, without an overly programmatic approach. But over and over again, I see people in our church open up their homes to strangers and outcasts. It's astonishing to me just how often this happens in our community without any prompting or formal facilitation from our leadership. It is very beautiful, and I have come to see that it is not at all fragile. There is hard-nosed love that underwrites what's happening here, a love that makes me want to take off my shoes in recognition of the holiness of it all.

These are the people who are taking me by the hand and pulling me into freedom today.

The un-ideal Christian community

One of the things that drew Blake (and many others) to our community was the way she experienced people really looking out for each other—and really looking out for her. What made her want to stay was the willingness of people like Dennis and Elizabeth to risk involvement in the messy, real lives of the people around them. And it's not just her; we've heard this many times. Doesn't that just make you want to move to Charlotte and join our church?

Before you put your house on the market, you need to hear this next part. I could also point you to plenty of people who got disillusioned at Renovatus in all the ways people get disillusioned in other churches. They didn't feel as if their gifts were cultivated, or they felt unnoticed (perhaps even by me). There was a personality conflict, or something they didn't like about my preaching or our leadership culture or the music. The people, incidentally, who are likely to leave our church the fastest are the same ones who have entered it the most enthusiastically. "This is the church I've always dreamed of. You are the best preacher I've ever heard. I won't leave this place until the day I die." Inevitably, those who come in with the highest expectations get disillusioned the fastest.

There is no gathering of people who meet in the name of Jesus, however formally or informally, that is not messy, and no relationship that is not complex. I'm part of conversations all the time in which people tell me some variation of, "I love Jesus, but I just don't love the church." I, of all people, understand that. I have a ringside seat for all sorts of nastiness and perplexity in the name of Jesus. Though I have beautiful stories of people like Margaret Gaines in my life, I also have plenty of stories about how broken the people of God can be. I sometimes feel more of a kinship with the sons and daughters who have been burned and become disillusioned with the church than with those who, like me, have never left the back porch. I share many of their feelings and experiences. I think I understand disillusioned people better than those who are not. When you've been scarred by encounters with crazy Christians, or find yourself inexplicably drawn to the person of Jesus despite the rather absurd people who seem to think they are conducting His business in the world, it really is tempting to ask, "Can't I just have a relationship with Jesus and not the church?" Actually, no. You can't.

I remember hearing Stanley Hauerwas's response when he was asked why he had stayed in the United Methodist Church for so long when he could be so savagely critical of it at times. "I've just always believed you stay with the people who have marked you," he responded. And that sums it up for me. Whatever failings the church might have, it's still my church. Everybody has a crazy uncle you'd like to hide somewhere when you bring your new girlfriend home from college to meet everybody, but you don't uninvite him from Thanksgiving dinner. He's crazy, but he's still your uncle. I'm also increasingly aware of the likelihood that I'm a crazy uncle in somebody else's life.

We've seen how beautiful it can be to follow Jesus into this new way of being human. But one of the things I love most about Jesus is how much He loves humanity in its brokenness. If He was surrounded by fractured people then, why would we expect it to be any different now? I actually think it is a larger mistake when we Christians attempt to pretend that our lives are more together than they really are in order to "manage our image" before the broader culture. *Come look at our perfect church and our perfect family. And if you join us, maybe one day you, too, can have a perfect life!* That kind of spin is a breeding ground for disappointment.

I love the work of the late Dominican priest Herbert McCabe. When a close friend of his decided to leave the Catholic church in demonstrative fashion because of "all the corruption," McCabe, as editor of a Catholic journal, wrote a critical editorial in which he said, "Of course it's corrupt. But that's no reason to leave it."[1]

I haven't stayed in the "institutional church" because I think it's not corrupt. As with any human system, disappointment is part and parcel of our life together—we all get disappointed and do some disappointing of our own. I just don't think it's a good reason to leave. And I still think the best thing for most of us is to find a Christian community somewhere that is kind of beautiful in all the ways that churches are often beautiful and ugly in all the ways that churches are often ugly, and get to work.

We have a document called the Renovatus Manifesto that we live by at our church—it's a declaration of what we believe is distinct about our community. Here is one of the statements: "We *are* your grandmother's church. And your great-grandmother's church. And your great-great-grandmother's church."

I had grown weary of the clichéd church advertising that said, "We aren't your grandmother's church." I understand what they mean by that. It's a way of saying that our church has electric guitars rather than pipe organs. I didn't grow up in churches with pipe organs, so I have no reason to be defensive about them now. Nevertheless, I couldn't help but be annoyed with the careless language. The desire to cut ourselves off from those who came before us is no virtue. Even when we are flatly, and perhaps rightly, embarrassed by the behavior or the history of our churches on some level, we still exist in continuity with them. We are forever tethered to our grandmother's church, and this is as it should be. Our grandmother's church has given us many good gifts. But even when it has been very wrong, it still belongs to us.

There is no such thing as cutting ourselves off and starting over. (Even the Protestant Reformation didn't truly suc-
ceed in that.) The reality of being the body of Christ leaves
us deeply connected, even when we try to walk away and do
something different. Of course we would love a clean slate
from the mistakes and failures of our grandmother's church,
because we could pretend we are without sin. But when we
dissociate ourselves from even the negative parts of our
respective church traditions, we are no longer conducting
our ministry from a starting place of repentance. And how
could that ever be a good idea?

I have never been able to shake Dietrich Bonhoeffer's
words on the subject of disillusionment in his powerful
little book *Life Together*:

> Just as surely as God desires to lead us to a knowl-
> edge of genuine Christian fellowship, so surely must
> we be overwhelmed by a great disillusionment with
> others, with Christians in general, and, if we are
> fortunate, with ourselves. . . .
>
> The sooner this shock of disillusionment comes
> to an individual and to a community, the better for
> both. A community which cannot bear and cannot
> survive such a crisis, which insists upon keeping its
> illusion when it should be shattered, permanently
> loses in that moment the promise of Christian
> community. Sooner or later it will collapse. Every
> human wish dream that is injected into the Christian

community is a hindrance to genuine community and must be banished if genuine community is to survive. He who loves his dream of a community more than the Christian community itself becomes a destroyer of the latter, even though his personal intentions may be ever so honest and earnest and sacrificial.

God hates visionary dreaming; it makes the dreamer proud and pretentious. The man who fashions a visionary ideal of community demands that it be realized by God, by others, and by himself. He enters the community of Christians with his demands, sets up his own law, and judges the brethren and God Himself accordingly. He stands adamant, a living reproach to all others in the circle of brethren. He acts as if he is the creator of the Christian community, as if his dream binds men together. When things do not go his way, he calls the effort a failure. When his ideal picture is destroyed, he sees the community going to smash. So he becomes, first an accuser of his brethren, then an accuser of God, and finally the despairing accuser of himself. . . .

When the morning mists of dreams vanish, then dawns the bright day of Christian fellowship.[2]

It is true that stepping into Christian community entails considerable risk. Because it is *human* community, there will be betrayal, disappointment, and heartbreak. Until the Son of Love comes again to complete the restoration He began in us, this will always be the case. We will get hurt, and at times we will do the hurting. And yet what a gift the people of God are to receive, and what a gift it is to be part of the people of God.

Even now, having just a small glimpse into how desperately loved I am by God, I'm convinced there is no way that I would know the dance, if not for my community. I would still hear the music, but there are far too many forces of fear and anxiety and self-consciousness that would keep me in my seat. Even now, I need somebody to love me enough to take me by the hand and lead me into the joyful celebration of my belovedness. That is what Christian community is all about.

9
witness

✧ ✧ ✧

*Sin consists in ceasing to reach out, refusing to respond
to the Father's summons, and settling for this present
world. What makes it possible for us to reach out, to
hear and respond to the summons, is that through the
resurrection of Christ the future world is already with
us as a disruptive force disturbing the order of the
world. We are able to some extent to live into the mode
of communication that belongs to the future world, the
mode we call charity or the presence of the Spirit.*

HERBERT MCCABE,
LAW, LOVE AND LANGUAGE

When Jesus touches our eyes, we are able to see many beautiful things in the world. The world around us is blazing
with the beauty of God. In the words of the psalmist, "The
earth is the LORD's, and the fulness thereof" (Psalm 24:1,
KJV). Within our bodies and the bodies of the people of
God around us, the seeds of resurrection are already bursting with life. In our own stories and the stories of those we
love, there are so many beautiful things to see.

And yet we ache for something more. The earth itself is longing for its intended beauty to be fully restored. When we see the ways in which the world is disjointed from the way it was intended to be, we enter into the dissonant dirge of the creation crying out. For me, I want to go back to the tabernacle where I first met with God, or I want to experience the joy and beauty of my grandmother's house. We long for restoration, not escape. We long for a world renewed and restored. The longing of God Himself to make the creation whole lingers in our dreams, pulling us forward, drawing us toward the good future He has in store for us and for the world.

The song we have inside us constantly comes into conflict with the violence, corruption, and inequality in the world. If we listen attentively to the Spirit, we hear God singing. If we listen a little bit closer, we hear Him weeping.

With the tension churning within us, knowing all the ways the earth is not yet as God intended it to be, we are driven to pray daily: "Thy kingdom come, Thy will be done in earth, as it is in heaven."[1] We are not looking for an escape from the world; we are looking for the restoration of the world. We are looking for the day when we meet the rightful Lord of the universe at the gates of the city and our absurd misfit parade becomes a processional for a King to bring His peaceful rule to the earth. We are looking for the day described in Revelation 21, when the new Jerusalem comes down.

Patiently, hopefully, actively we are waiting for Jesus.

And yet here is the astonishing twist: As we wait for our Lord and the bodily resurrection yet to come for the departed, the world waits for us. As we long for God, the world is longing for God in us.

In the same section of the book of Romans where Paul describes the earth's travail, he includes a curious line: "The creation waits with eager longing for the revealing of the children of God" (Romans 8:19). As we have already seen, we have become the body of Christ for the world. The same Spirit who raised Him from the dead is at work in us—we are now authorized to speak on His behalf, to touch on His behalf.

The same splendid terror of resurrection at work in Jesus will one day be released into the entire cosmos, and the creation will be restored. But in the meantime, within our own bruised and broken bodies, something of that restoration is already at work in the earth. What the world needs now are signposts of what's ahead, markers for the new world just around the corner. The world does not need heroes; the world does not need more messiah complexes. The world does not need Christians who want to ride in on a white horse to save the day. What the world needs are *witnesses*. Nothing more and nothing less. The earth needs people who can bear witness to the ways in which the world has already changed through the resurrection of Jesus of Nazareth.

Where will we find these witnesses?

When the Holy Ghost sent me to Memphis

All the way back to when I was the boy on the bike, I felt drawn to the life and legacy of Dr. Martin Luther King Jr. When I was in the seventh grade at Charlotte's Wilson Middle School, the school system facilitated a poetry contest for students in honor of Martin Luther King Day. I am surprised to realize that I more or less remember the poem I entered, even though I don't have an actual copy anywhere:

> *In a land in a storm*
> *Of fury and hate*
> *Stepped out a man*
> *Who opened a gate*
> *Of freedom and faith*
> *For all mankind.*
> *Though misunderstood,*
> *His faith he would not resign,*
> *Until he showed us the truth*
> *We did not want to find.*
> *With visions of peace and strength to love,*
> *He showed us the way that came from above.*

I feel as if I'm missing a section, but it was something like that, anyway. As you can surmise, I didn't have much of a future as a poet. Winning second place in that contest was the height of my poetic career. But the poem does bring me back to a time in my life when I was captivated by the dream of Martin Luther King with an ideological purity and simplicity that is difficult to recapture as an adult. It reflects the pureness of heart of the boy on the bike.

I wasn't very knowledgeable about King's life or legacy then, but I knew enough to know that his message was deeply related to the gospel I learned and the Jesus I loved. When you're in seventh grade, it's easy to dream big and dream out loud about the world you want to live in. Cynicism is the most insidious of demons and one of the first we have to stare down. But at age twelve, I had not yet faced that demon.

Last summer my wife and I were supposed to fly from Denver to Nashville via Atlanta. Because of a storm in Atlanta, the airport was closed and our flight was routed to Memphis instead. But with no more flights to Nashville after we landed, Amanda and I ended up with a free day in Memphis. On a whim, we decided to go to the Lorraine Motel, the site where Dr. King was killed, which is now the National Civil Rights Museum.

Not unlike my experience after my prayer with Jim that led to my boy on a bike encounter, this was the second time within a few months when I felt God bring something full circle in my life. In recent years, I've had the opportunity to go to a lot of traditional Christian holy sites all over the Middle East and Rome. But in none of those places, nor in any church building, had I ever experienced anything quite like what I did in Memphis.

After Amanda and I ate fried chicken at Gus's, we took a leisurely walk to the Lorraine. As soon as we turned the corner and were able to see the hotel balcony where King was shot, I was overcome by the presence of God. I don't know if that sounds weird to you, but it was intense and it was very much like the feeling I had on my Seabrook Island bike ride. A sacred hush fell between Amanda and me. And then we began to weep at the same time. I was undone. I've never felt God's presence attached to a physical space like I did at the Lorraine Motel.

As we walked into the museum, we intended to take a quick look and be on our way. Though our tickets gave us access to the screening of a free film, we planned to skip it. But when the announcement came over the loudspeaker that the film was about to start, I felt a strong inward prompting, in no uncertain terms, that I must go watch the film. I knew it was God, but I didn't understand why or how such a thing would matter.

At the time, I was preaching a series on the book of Revelation at our church, and my next sermon was supposed to be about the enigmatic "two witnesses" in Revelation 11. The two witnesses are killed and then resurrected after three and a half days, and in their death and resurrection, God accomplishes victory in the world.

So as I settled in to watch the film—*The Witness: From the Balcony of Room 306*—I felt God's message already burning in my heart. The documentary tells the story of the Rev. Samuel "Billy" Kyles, one of the last living witnesses to have shared the final hour of Dr. King's life inside the Lorraine Motel. He describes Dr. King's mental state as he preached his epic "I've Been to the Mountaintop" sermon the night before he was shot. In words I'll never forget, Kyles said, "That night, he preached himself through the fear of death."

In the film footage of the speech, Dr. King says, "You can kill this dreamer . . . but you cannot kill his dream." When I heard those words, the truth of the Cross came alive to me like never before. The story of the death and resurrection of Jesus is the story of Martin Luther King Jr. and the story of all faithful witnesses.

I wept throughout the film and couldn't leave my seat when it was over. As Billy Kyles told his story of being a witness to Dr. King's death, the reality of Revelation's message settled over me in a whole new way. We are those who bear witness to the victory God has achieved through the death and resurrection of Jesus of Nazareth. Our message is not our own; like Billy Kyles, we bear witness to one greater than ourselves.

There were many ways in which God used Martin Luther King to change the world. Books such as Charles Marsh's wonderful *The Beloved Community: How Faith Shapes Social Justice, from the Civil Rights Movement to Today* and Richard Lischer's marvelous *The Preacher King: Martin Luther King Jr. and the Word that Moved America* bear witness. They make the case brilliantly that Dr. King and the civil rights movement cannot be understood apart from their explicit grounding in Christianity and its vivid biblical imagery. King himself, though he experienced a martyr's death, bore witness to one greater than himself.

Martin Luther King preached the gospel of the Kingdom of God. That was his primary message. He just applied it to a very particular area of racial and economic injustice. He had heard many black preachers distract their congregations from the woes of the present world to talk about a distant heaven in another land for another time. But King himself was seized by the immediacy of the Kingdom message:

> It's all right to talk about streets flowing with milk and honey, but God has commanded us to be concerned about the slums down here and His children who can't eat three square meals a day. It's all right to talk about the new Jerusalem, but one day, God's preacher must talk about the new New York, the new Atlanta, the new Philadelphia, the new Los Angeles, the new Memphis, Tennessee. This is what we have to do.[2]

Now and then we've seen glimpses of the new Charlotte around here. Mat Rogers does communications and graphic design for Renovatus by day, but his real passion in life is for the folks in the apartments at Birchcroft, the most ethnically diverse and densely populated little space in our city. The landlords get a tax credit for placing international residents there, so there is a remarkable blend of cultures—people from Somalia and Nepal and Vietnam.

A few Saturdays ago, I was out at Birchcroft with our

volunteers. Some of our guys were there from our car care ministry, fixing cars free of charge. Some were part of a team going around and cleaning apartments. Some of us went door-to-door handing out bouquets of flowers, just as a way of saying, "We love you and think you are beautiful." And it's not just handouts—a few weeks ago, we hosted an on-site job fair to get Birchcroft residents connected with small business owners. As we went from house to house, we often couldn't speak the language of the residents. Our Nepali translator came late. But no matter—the message was emblazed in the tenderness of our face-to-face contacts. In this little pocket of our city, we are quite literally seeing God's Kingdom come.

Martin Luther King heard the music. He was one of those exiles of our time who was willing to "come up here"[3] to receive a different vision of the world, to see the world not for what it is but what it is called to be. As it was in those brief moments when the earth convulsed and dead bodies were walking around Jerusalem as a precursor to the great resurrection yet to come,[4] Dr. King caught a glimpse of the promise of creation renewed.

Revelation is a book full of martyrs who share in the victory of the Lamb of God on the cross. They are those who have "conquered . . . by the blood of the Lamb and by the word of their testimony, for they did not cling to life even in the face of death" (Revelation 12:11).

In this book, I have attempted to bear witness. I have told you my story. But I also believe that my story bears witness to a greater story—the story of the death and resurrection of

Jesus. I believe you, too, have a story to tell: a story of your belovedness. It's a story of how your scars and wounds and death fit into the story of the death of Jesus, of how your victories fit into the victory of God's love over the power of death. I believe that you, too, are called to "follow the Lamb wherever he goes" (Revelation 14:4), telling your story, allowing His wounds to heal your own, clinging not to your own life even in the face of death.

Your story is not just your own. It is part of something bigger. It is part of the story of how God wants to establish "the new New York, the new Atlanta, the new Philadelphia, the new Los Angeles, the new Memphis, Tennessee." This is what we have to do. Like Martin Luther King's "beloved community," we've got to get in with a group of people who are willing to astonish this present world, in its loneliness and disconnection, with the peace and joy that comes from the future. We've got to be part of a community that will show the world through our love one for another the beautiful things God has in store for His creation.

I'd love to talk about how God wants to touch you, but you're no charity case. Do you understand where all of this has been going? God wants to touch others through you. The sensuous Lord of dirt, this sweaty God, is still present by His Spirit, and He wants to touch broken people through your touch. The ancient song throbs through creation, desperate for renewal. Romans 8:19 says that "the creation waits with eager longing for the *revealing of the children of God*" (emphasis added). Now do you understand why it's so important for you to grasp your belovedness? God won't change the world through angels or through ideas; He will change the world through His sons and daughters. If you don't know who you are, if you don't know your true identity, you won't touch others on His behalf.

The time has come for the revelation of the boys on the bikes and the girls on the trampolines. God wants to show you off. He loves you and delights in you simply because you exist. There is something unique you have to do for Him in establishing His futuristic Kingdom of peace in the world. We have the prototype, Jesus, who has shown us the way. It's time for each one of us to embrace the identity we were given before the world was made. He wants to make our wounds a resource for the healing of others. He wants to make His resurrection power known through our real, day-to-day lives. Do you have any idea what's at stake in your understanding who you really are?

Everyone is afraid of the apocalypse; everyone is afraid of the end of the world. But the old world ends and the new one begins when you finally awake to hear your true name. Arise from your slumber, beloved. The future is at hand.

No wonder Matthew's account of Jesus' death and resurrection is filled with apocalyptic language—from that day forward, the future has been barreling down on us. When I was growing up, we asked a lot of questions about what was going to happen in the future. But the question the Gospels ultimately pose is this: *What are we going to do now that God's future is crashing into the present?*

An invitation: "Come up here"

Like you, I have days when life feels difficult and sometimes wearying. Pastoral ministry is largely an indoor sport, and it is easy for me to get out of rhythm with the song of creation.

But every now and then, I hear a playful whisper coming from outside:

"Come up here . . ."

These are the very words John heard while exiled on the island of Patmos, when God called him to see the world from a different vantage point. He saw and heard the same story we get from the Law and the Prophets to the Gospels and the Epistles, but it's the entire story from an aerial perspective.

"Come up here . . ."

All you who are dizzy and road weary from the tedious talk of right and left and conservative and liberal and success and failure, come with me. There is yet a world where tyrants are overthrown and the oppressed are exalted and playfulness trumps toil and love trumps hate and imagination trumps pragmatism and white horses trump Cadillacs, a world where Jesus calls the shots. It's neither spiritual nor hidden nor distant, but palpable and present, and just around the corner.

"Come up here . . ."

To every bleary-eyed wanderer who looks at a world in which violence seems to triumph over peace and anger triumphs over tenderness and injustice over justice, I say come with me. Come and see that the lion is actually a lamb and dying is actually winning.

"Come up here . . ."

It's the same vision the prophet Isaiah saw of the restoration of all things, of the Son of Love coming to make all the wrongs in the world right again. It's the same vision that has captured every great witness, including Margaret Gaines and Dr. Martin Luther King Jr. In the words of Isaiah 11:6-9,

> The wolf shall live with the lamb,
>> the leopard shall lie down with the kid,
> the calf and the lion and the fatling together,
>> and a little child shall lead them.
> The cow and the bear shall graze,
>> their young shall lie down together;
>> and the lion shall eat straw like the ox.
> The nursing child shall play over the hole of the asp,
>> and the weaned child shall put its hand on the
>>> adder's den.
> They will not hurt or destroy on all my holy
>> mountain;
> for the earth will be full of the knowledge of
>> the Lord
>> as the waters cover the sea.

Can you see that's where the music has been headed all along?

letter to a ravaged bride

In this book, I have not attempted to say anything novel. Though the language of Jesus as prototype for a new way of being human may seem provocative, it is less so than the New Testament language of Jesus as the "firstborn from the dead" (Colossians 1:18). Our individual stories are now part of a larger story, the story of the church. We are the community of new humans entrusted with the task of making the future present.

If you can bear witness to the kinds of lives described in this book, I celebrate that. But my fear is that many Christians have not yet seen this kind of witness. The church has been entrusted with the sacred responsibility of being the broken and beautiful people of God for the world. But I understand this is not always the case. All too often, we have not been witnesses to the future. We don't always act as if we believe that Jesus has already changed the world. We are still the bride of Christ, but we are a ravaged bride.

I make no apologies for the brokenness of God's people, nor my own. It is as true of the church at large as it is for me as an individual—I am so broken, and yet so beloved. Nonetheless, I long for the day when the church can again understand the unique power that has been given to us. I long for the day when we see the life and words of Jesus as the model for our own. There are times when the combination of frustration and desire boils over in my life.

It's true that the best thing we can do is learn how to embrace and be embraced in an imperfect Christian community. But I want to close with a challenge to those who are already connected to such a community. We must live up to the calling that has been placed on us, to once again become the beautiful people of God for the world.

I was struggling deeply with these very issues about a year ago when I came home late one night and wrote the following letter. It feels as relevant now as ever:

To a Ravaged Bride (somewhere in America):

I could pretend I don't love you anymore. I could yell and scream and break things. I could dramatically walk out—like you and I are on a movie set—and say something pious as I slam the door. I could manufacture looks of disgust, or better yet, I could turn my eyes away. But you know me too well, don't you? You know that even when I'm petty or enraged, even when I lash out at you with self-righteous indignation (is there any other kind?)—you always have my heart. Even when you are in tatters, your gown ripped and your makeup smeared, a clownish parody of what you once were—you are still beautiful.

So I write to you less as a scorned lover, and more as a heartsick old fool, wearing my displaced affections like medals. And I want to talk to you with the detached wisdom of a professor or the elegant rhythm of a poet, but I always end up stammering when I'm close to you. Why should I bother to go through the machinations of fury and distance when you see through me every time? You see me wearing my rage and my confidence like a silly fake mustache, a failed disguise for my broken heart.

So I'm writing to you today, honestly trying to avoid bravado and forced swagger, knowing that we are in this together—I am in you and you are in me. I want to write you off; I want to cut you down to size. I want to tell you that you cannot be the bride Christ came to save, to tell you that you missed Him already and that He's moved on to a more authentic love. But I know that you are still the bride, and I know He hasn't moved on from you. So I'm stuck here, chained to the radiator, loving you partly under compulsion and partly from real tenderness.

You're still seductively pretty. But for the life of me I can't figure out what's happened to you, to your charm and courage and grace under pressure. There's a mad and hopelessly wonderful jungle around your house, full of danger and opportunity. Why are you trying to burn it down? You used to know that when the people around you were at their angriest and everybody was looking for someone to stone—you would just go walking past with no weapon but your own fragrant perfume. You didn't just charm, you disarmed—you could walk through a room and make it go silent, save for the clang of swords dropping to the ground. You brought tenderness into the war zone and wine to the party. What happened to you to make you start acting like *them*—screaming and demanding and posturing?

You still look the same from a distance, but up close I know something is badly wrong. Something is different this time around. I'm not sure I know who you are. Whenever I'm at denominational meetings and we are trying to find someone to blame for our sinking ship, I don't just see the individuals. I see you in all of your collective horror. I've seen your outrage at political rallies, festivities that talk about "values" without words like *Kingdom* or *Cross*. I heard your protests when "they" started infringing on our territory (Muslims and Mexicans and lions and tigers and bears, oh my), and you felt as if you needed to stand up to them instead of laying down your life for them. I noticed when your rhetoric went from "good news" to yet another brand of paranoid propaganda.

Let's not be coy here, honey. We've lived together for too long, and we know each other's secrets and habits and fears. We share ideas and we share clothes; we drink from the same cup. But did you think no one would notice that your knuckles started getting bloodier than your palms? That the blood on your hands was theirs and not yours?

It's not that I think you don't still have answers. It's not that the world outside needs you any less. But right now the chemo seems more toxic than the cancer, baby. We came here to this place to lay down our lives, but the corpses in the backyard are more from our swords than from our crosses.

Do you think me naive? You think I don't know there's an enemy to fight? On the contrary, my love. I've seen the monsters under the bed. I know that there is a force of evil in the world that is greater than the sum of its parts. I know we've got dragons to slay. It's just that they don't scare me.

In the words of Bob Dylan, "Let us not talk falsely now, the hour is getting late."[1] So I'll risk more honesty than can typically be afforded on an average Sunday:

I know the world is a volatile, dangerous place. There is a part of me, cold and scientific, that expects the world to blow itself up. It's not prophecy; it's pure arithmetic. We are endlessly creative in finding new ways to conquer and destroy. The more people learn to manipulate chemicals and machines, the worse our chances become.

But if I'm honest, that doesn't really scare me either. If more war breaks out tomorrow and the rocket's red glare becomes nuclear, and dirty bombs are bursting in air, and half of creation is maimed— I still believe that the creative power of divine love would rise from the ashes. God already died. Terrorism is not nearly as frightening as blood and water gushing from the side of the Creator, and even that terror of terrors was swept up in resurrection life. I am not afraid of the horrible things human beings might do to me or to one another.

But I am afraid of you—still a mighty power in the universe, still the world's great hope. You are still the church. Nobody has the power to create or destroy quite like you. Sometimes we have seen the world around us exploding, and when we do, we groan with the creation for the restoration that is to come. But what if you go up in flames? What if the salt loses its savor? What if you, a once chaste and patient virgin, take the oil from your own lamp, and throw it in someone else's face—and strike the match? The apostle Paul said that the weapons of our warfare are not carnal, but mighty in God. But you've been firing them in the dense fog; you don't know who or what you are aiming at. You've been flailing punches instead of turning the other cheek.

God help us, you've been beating your plowshares into swords.

You know I'm no cynic—I've loved you too long for that. This is love animated by grief. I still believe in you despite all of your vices. You can still dazzle me. You can still dazzle the world, bride of God. But things are feeling as insane in here as they are out there, honey. And I don't know what else to do except to remind you of the time when you were lovely.

Jonathan

acknowledgments

While this is not a memoir per se, so much of my story and the beautiful story of the people of Renovatus is wrapped up in these pages. In an odd way, this sums up everything I've learned about God, life, and the world in thirty-four years. As such, all the people who have most shaped my life have most shaped this book. But here are a few people I especially want to thank, many of whom you've met in the preceding pages.

My wife, Amanda: So many of these ideas have been forged over the course of thousands of hours of conversations with you. I wouldn't have a story to tell apart from you. Thank you for accommodating yourself to life with a mad scientist and being my live-in editor. People laugh when I say that you do the praying and I do the preaching, but I'm afraid it's more true than they could know. I get to be the front man, but the highest compliment I can give is that you're the person I'd most want to be my pastor. I love you.

My executive pastor, Tracey Rouse (aka the girl on the trampoline): Every single time I hit a roadblock with this project, you not only found the way out, you did so with dazzling ease. You are smart in all the ways I am not and could never be. I could not have made it past chapter 3 without you, much less run a church. And I wouldn't want to try, you know?

My assistant, Elizabeth Donahue: You bring so much class to our team and to my life, and you and Dennis take care of me like I'm your own. You are a gracious gift to us.

The remarkable staff of Renovatus Church: Blake, Sarah, Teddy (Rondo!) and Krystle, Jonathan, Mat, Chris, Jake, Chuck and Teresa, Aaron and Tracy, Broderick and Mona, and Vic—this is your story as much as it is mine.

My amazing friends: To Nathan Rouse, who has shared more than a decade of Buechner and *X-Files* and U2 shows and highly inappropriate jokes—your own courageous vision for faith and the arts continues to inspire me. Clayton King, the big brother I never had—thank you for always having my back. Steven Furtick, my most generous friend—you have always, always believed in me and spoken life into me. Jim Driscoll, a true elder in my life—thank you for caring so well for my soul. Dr. Chris Green, my new old friend, for pushing me over the ledge to fully embrace the centrality of the Table.

Jan Long Harris, my editor Dave Lindstedt, and my new family at Tyndale: Thank you for taking a chance on an unknown. From the first time I met you guys, I was moved by your heart for ministry, the sense of community on your team, and your passion for this project. It's an honor to do this with you.

My agent, David Van Diest: We've come a long way! Thanks for all your encouragement.

The Renovatus elders: Thank you for always lifting my arms when they are weary.

The entire community at Renovatus: I have the best gig in the world, and I am so honored that you call me your pastor. I hope these pages demonstrate all the ways I've been your student.

I'd also like to thank the people who have most directly shaped how I see the world—my mentors and spiritual fathers and mothers: Margaret Gaines, Rickie Moore, Cheryl and Jackie Johns, John Christopher Thomas, Steven J. Land, and Stanley Hauerwas. I'd also like to thank Dr. Corrine Goodwin for all the ways she has helped keep me sane during this season—a considerable feat.

My old friends who've stuck by me: Especially Reed Lackey, for his valuable insight on the early manuscript, and Dave Galloway, who was there for me even during the awkward years.

My beautiful family: Jess, Rita, and Zachary—thanks especially for the bike! It turned out to be a good investment, right?

And finally, to my mom and dad, Ronald and Lynda Martin, to whom this book is dedicated: There is absolutely no way I could be at this place in my life without your love and prayers. Everything I most needed to know about God I know from being your son.

notes

CHAPTER 1: IDENTITY

1. See, for example, Nicholas Carr, *The Shallows: What the Internet Is Doing to Our Brains* (New York: Norton, 2011).
2. Sherry Turkle, *Alone Together: Why We Expect More from Technology and Less from Each Other* (New York: Basic, 2011), 153.
3. Henri Nouwen's phrase from *The Inner Voice of Love: A Journey through Anguish to Freedom* (New York: Doubleday, 1998).

CHAPTER 2: BELOVED

1. Bruce Springsteen, "Devils and Dust," 2005.
2. See Ephesians 6:12, KJV.
3. John O'Donohue, interview with Krista Tippett on October 1, 2007; broadcast on the February 28, 2008, edition of the radio program *Speaking of Faith*, from American Public Media. A transcript of the conversation can be found at "The Inner Landscape of Beauty," *On Being* with Krista Tippett (blog), January 26, 2012, http://www.onbeing.org/program/inner-landscape-beauty/transcript/1125.
4. Eugene H. Peterson, *Leap Over a Wall: Earthy Spirituality for Everyday Christians* (New York: HarperCollins, 1997), 115.
5. Henri J. M. Nouwen, *Here and Now: Living in the Spirit* (New York: Crossroad Publishing, 1994), 165. Nouwen continues, "We are God's beloved daughters and sons, not because we have proven ourselves worthy of God's love, but because God freely chose us. It is very hard to stay in touch with our true identity because those who want our money, our time, and our energy profit more from our insecurity and fears than from our inner freedom."
6. U2, "Beautiful Day," 2000.

7. Ibid.
8. John 1:29, ESV
9. Mark 1:11
10. Hebrews 4:15, NKJV

CHAPTER 3: OBSCURITY
1. Sherry Turkle, *Alone Together: Why We Expect More from Technology and Less from Each Other* (New York: Basic, 2011), xii.
2. Ibid.
3. Ibid., 17.

CHAPTER 4: CALLING
1. Mark 8:24
2. Thomas Merton, *Conjectures of a Guilty Bystander* (New York: Doubleday Religion, 1965), 140–141.
3. The text of this account, found in Luke 7:36-50 and parallel passages, does not explicitly state that the woman was a prostitute. But it is a common assumption in church tradition, and it certainly fits the profile of the kinds of people Jesus associated with.

CHAPTER 5: WOUNDS
1. Galatians 6:17; see also 2 Corinthians 4:10.
2. Isaiah 53:3-5

CHAPTER 6: RESURRECTION
1. See John 21:9.
2. See Luke 24:13-31.
3. Rowan Williams, *Tokens of Trust: An Introduction to Christian Belief* (Louisville, KY: Westminster John Knox, 2007), 21–22.
4. Margaret Gaines, speaking at Renovatus, October 2008.
5. Ibid.
6. Ibid.
7. Phrase adapted from Elizabeth Barrett Browning's poem "Aurora Leigh," from the section that says, ""Earth's crammed with heaven,/And every common bush afire with God,/But only he who sees takes off his shoes;/ The rest sit round and pluck blackberries."

CHAPTER 7: SACRAMENTS
1. Exodus 19:16-18
2. Frederick Buechner, *Secrets in the Dark: A Life in Sermons* (San Francisco: HarperOne, 2006), 135.

3. Matthew 17:1-7
4. Stanley Hauerwas, *Disrupting Time: Sermons, Prayers, and Sundries* (Eugene, OR: Cascade, 2004), 127.
5. John 14:16, KJV
6. Sherry Turkle, *Alone Together: Why We Expect More from Technology and Less from Each Other* (New York: Basic, 2011), 11-12.
7. Wallace Shawn and Andre Gregory, *My Dinner with Andre*, copyright © 1981 The André Company. A transcript of the screenplay can be found online at http://www.cloudnet.com/~jwinder/dinner.htm.
8. Chris Hedges, *Empire of Illusion: The End of Literacy and the Triumph of Spectacle* (New York: Nation, 2009), 57.
9. Ibid., 82.
10. Shawn and Gregory, *My Dinner with Andre*.
11. Marilynne Robinson, *Gilead* (New York: Picador, 2004), 17.
12. Ibid.
13. Ibid.
14. Ibid., 18.
15. Herbert McCabe, *Law, Love and Language* (New York: Continuum, 2003), 152–153.
16. David Bowie, "Space Oddity," 1969.
17. Richard B. Hays, *Interpretation: First Corinthians* (Louisville, KY: Westminster John Knox, 1997), 196–197.
18. I don't know where we originally found this invitation, but it is readily available online. I have heard it attributed to a Communion liturgy from the Iona Community in Scotland but have not found a citable source.
19. 1 Corinthians 15:45, ESV

CHAPTER 8: COMMUNITY

1. I first heard this story from Stanley Hauerwas. As he tells it, the Catholic Church responded to McCabe's editorial by removing him from his post as editor. After a season away, he was allowed to resume his job. In his first editorial after his return, McCabe began with the line, "Before I was so strangely interrupted . . ."
2. Dietrich Bonhoeffer, *Life Together* (New York: HarperCollins, 1954), 26–29.

CHAPTER 9: WITNESS

1. Matthew 6:10, KJV
2. Dr. Martin Luther King Jr., "I've Been to the Mountaintop," sermon at Bishop Charles Mason Temple, Memphis, Tennessee, April 3, 1968.

A transcript of the sermon can be viewed online at http://mlk-kpp01
.stanford.edu/index.php/encyclopedia/documentsentry/ive_been_to
_the_mountaintop.

3. Revelation 4:1
4. Matthew 27:51-53

EPILOGUE: LETTER TO A RAVAGED BRIDE

1. Bob Dylan, "All Along the Watchtower," copyright © 1968, 1996 by
Dwarf Music.

discussion guide

This discussion guide is designed for a four-week group study of *Prototype*. Within each week, the questions are broken out by chapter so you can adjust for a shorter or longer study as best fits your needs. Feel free to focus on the questions or issues that resonate the most with your group; the guide is intended to be a starting point for deeper conversation, community, and spiritual growth, so use it as a base and let God guide your time together.

Week one: Read chapters 1 and 2

Chapter 1: Identity

1. Jonathan Martin tells his story of being "the boy on the bike" and his friend's story of being "the girl on the trampoline." Think back over your life—how would you describe who you were at the time when you were most purely and naturally connected to God?

2. Read Mark 5:1-20. What does Jonathan identify about the crowd's fear? Do you agree "it is much scarier to encounter people who are sane"? Can you think of another biblical example of this?

3. Why does Jonathan think people who come to understand God's love for them describe the feeling as a *homecoming*? Consider a time when you "came home" and what it felt like; how does your experience compare to Jonathan's description?

4. Jonathan admits he doesn't often feel like he's "together" enough to be a pastor. Can you relate to this admission? What qualities do you think are important for a pastor to have? Think about a key component of your own identity (parent, professional, sibling, child, colleague)—what qualities are important to your sense of identity? Do you always feel confident in them? How might your feelings change if you fully embraced your identity as God's beloved as Jonathan describes?

5. What if the ultimate goal of everything Jesus said and did was not just to get us to believe certain things about Him, but for us to *become* like Him? What would that look like in your life? How would it change the way you live?

Chapter 2: Beloved

1. Jonathan says he's "coming to believe that fear is at the heart of all sin and disaffection." Why is this so? What fears does he specifically highlight as examples? Do you believe it is ever appropriate, or good, to be afraid? Think about the fears in your own life—which category do they fall into? What would it feel like to be free of them?

2. When was the last time you stopped long enough to enjoy and appreciate the beauty of nature or music or art? When was the last time you felt truly and deeply loved? How would you describe that feeling?

3. Read David's description of God's love in Psalm 139:1-18. Which verses speak to you the most? What do they mean to you?

4. What does Jonathan say is the most pronounced difference between David's and Saul's early lives, and how did it affect them? Which one bears more resemblance to your own childhood? What impact would you say this aspect of your life has had on your understanding of and relationship to God?

5. What does Jonathan consider Jesus' defining moment that set the course for everything He would do and become? Have you had such a defining moment in your own life? If so, describe it. If not, what stops you from asking God for one?

Week two: Read chapters 3 and 4

Chapter 3: Obscurity

1. What does Jonathan define as "the wilderness" and what are its characteristics? Why might God call some people there? What would you tell someone who feels they are experiencing God's displeasure?

2. Jonathan says there is one way we can always identify the devil's voice. What is it? Do you agree or disagree? What do you think might help tune that voice out the next time you hear it?

3. What are your thoughts on technology, such as cell phones, e-mail, and social media? How much do you rely on them? Do you agree that part of the appeal is that they make us feel needed, important, and valuable? What might be positive and/or negative about that?

4. Would you say you are comfortable with silence? Explain. Do you have times of solitude with God? If so, what do you feel is the benefit? If not, how might you make time for solitude this week?

Chapter 4: Calling

1. Jonathan says, "It's always the most unlikely people who do the most astonishingly beautiful good work in God's Kingdom." What examples does he give? What others can you think of from Scripture, history, or your own life? What makes these people "unlikely" and how does God use them in spite of (or through) their perceived weaknesses? What is one of your own weaknesses that God has found a way to use for your calling?

2. Why is "liars, dreamers, and misfits" a special phrase to Jonathan? Think of the different kinds of community in your life and the people within them who are important to you. What words, lyrics, or phrases might you use to describe yourselves as a community?

3. Jonathan retells the biblical story of the woman who poured oil on Jesus' feet. Have you ever made an extravagant gesture to show God how much you love Him—and did others think you were crazy? Consider what might please God as a gift from your heart.

Week three: Read chapters 5, 6, and 7

Chapter 5: Wounds

1. "It's not exactly an icebreaker for a party," Jonathan acknowledges, "but if we really wanted to get to know each other, we would ask to see each other's scars." What are the potential benefits of allowing others to

know about the things that have hurt or damaged us?
What are the risks? In what ways do you consider Jesus
our prototype when it comes to being vulnerable about
his wounds?

2. Everyone knows what it is to be bullied, to be
displaced, to be labeled, to be left out. What does it
mean to you to have a God who experienced all of
those things? Can you think of any in your social circle
(at church, at work, etc.) whom you suspect might be
experiencing these feelings now? In what way might
you reach out to them this week and let them know
they're not alone?

3. Jonathan says, "One of my baseline assumptions about
ministry is that God is *already* wherever I'm headed, and
I'm just there to help folks recognize Him. . . . We
believed God's presence was strongly with us in the
same way He's present whenever anybody really loves
someone." How is this similar to or different from your
own beliefs and practices about sharing God's love with
others, particularly strangers?

4. Discuss Blake's story. Why does Jonathan say that
"sometimes the sacred thing . . . is simply to *shut up*"?
Have you ever found this to be true in your own life?
How was it true in his relationship with Blake?

5. What issues are you wrestling with right now? Reread
the verses at the end of this chapter and write down

these words: *Don't stop until the sun is up.* Put them in your car, on your fridge, in your Bible—somewhere you will see them every day. And hang on.

Chapter 6: Resurrection

1. Jonathan describes his experience of trying to get back to his grandmother's house. Think of a place from your past to which you'd like to go back. What made that place special or sacred to you?

2. "Resurrection changes everything." What does that phrase mean to you? What hopes or fears does it stir in your soul?

3. What is your reaction to the events described in Matthew 27? Do you agree with Jonathan that "if you find it simply comforting, you're not thinking about it hard enough"?

4. What does it tell you about the character of God that when doubters ask for proof, He is willing to deliver it?

Chapter 7: Sacraments

1. Why do you think Jesus so often used touch to heal?

2. What has been your own experience with baptism? Do you think there is a place for arguments over exactly what occurs in the act of baptism and how it should be expressed?

3. Why does Jonathan refer to acts such as foot washing and anointing with oil as "futuristic rites"? What about these acts makes them futuristic?

4. What do you think it means to "touch [someone] on God's behalf"? Was there a time in your life when you did this this or it was done to you?

5. Jonathan shares his childhood fear that God would smite him for not being holy enough for Communion. When you were a child, did you have any irrational fears or beliefs about God? How did they inform your faith journey?

Week four: Read chapters 8 and 9 and the epilogue

Chapter 8: Community

1. Have you ever been overcome in an unexpected way during a worship service? What about the experience moved, excited, unnerved, or energized you?

2. Name some reasons to "stay in the pew" and some to get out and dance.

3. What are some ways the Renovatus family cared for Dianne's soul through caring for her body? What were their risks in doing so? What do you think these actions showed Dianne about the way Jesus loves her?

4. Do you believe that the human body is sacred? How might your belief one way or the other inform your

views on social issues such as abortion, human trafficking, organ donation, the death penalty, treatment of prisoners, and others?

5. Do you think you can have a relationship with Jesus but not the church? Why or why not?

Chapter 9: Witness

1. Why does Jonathan say the world does not need heroes—it needs witnesses?

2. What examples does Jonathan give of witnesses? Who are others you might name?

3. What are some actions you might take to bring God's Kingdom to your own corner of community—your office or your neighborhood block?

4. Jonathan asks: "Do you have any idea what's at stake in your understanding who you really are?" What would he say is at stake? How would you answer his question today?

Epilogue: Letter to a Ravaged Bride

1. In his letter, Jonathan describes the church as a "ravaged bride." How would you describe it? If you were to write your own letter to the church at large, what would you want to say?

2. How does Jonathan's letter affect you? If you were to write him a response, what would you say to him?

about the author

Jonathan Martin leads the liars, dreamers, and misfits of Renovatus: A Church for People Under Renovation, in Charlotte, North Carolina, where he lives with his wife, Amanda. He's a product of the "Christ-haunted landscape" of the American South, sweaty revivals, and hip-hop. He holds degrees from Gardner-Webb University, Pentecostal Theological Seminary, and Duke University Divinity School. Jonathan's main claim to fame was getting his Aquaman, Robin, and Wonder Woman action figures saved, sanctified, and filled with the Holy Ghost at an early age. When he is talking, it's mostly about the beauty of God, what an extraordinary thing it is for us to be called God's beloved, and finding new ways to be human. He is unafraid to be seen walking his small dog, Cybil. For more information about Jonathan and his ministry, see pastorjonathanmartin.com.

Online Discussion *guide*

TAKE *your* TYNDALE READING
EXPERIENCE *to the* NEXT LEVEL

A FREE discussion guide for this book
is available at bookclubhub.net, perfect
for sparking conversations in your book
group or for digging deeper into the text
on your own.

www.bookclubhub.net

*You'll also find free discussion guides for
other Tyndale books, e-newsletters, e-mail
devotionals, virtual book tours, and more!*

FRESH AIR IS ABOUT TO SWEEP INTO YOUR LIFE.

This powerful debut book from Chris Hodges will revive your spirit and show you how to be fueled by God like never before. Take a deep breath of fresh air . . . and experience what it means to live an "I *get* to"— not an "I've *got* to"—kind of life every day.

Chris Hodges is being used by God in our generation to bring new insights and leadership to the church. Discover the powerful secrets of a God-breathed life and enjoy the fresh air of God's blessing.

STEVEN FURTICK
LEAD PASTOR, ELEVATION CHURCH; AUTHOR OF SUN STAND STILL
AND THE NEW YORK TIMES BESTSELLER GREATER

I love this book! Fresh Air will help you escape the mundane treadmill of living by empty rules and striving for empty success. With authenticity and clarity, Chris points us to the person who makes life fun again: Jesus.

JUDAH SMITH
LEAD PASTOR, THE CITY CHURCH

DO YOU HAVE THE COURAGE
TO FOLLOW JESUS INTO THE THICKET
OF HIS HEALING GRACE?

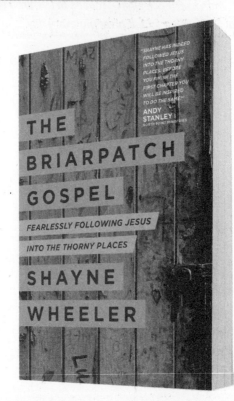

THE BRIARPATCH GOSPEL

FEARLESSLY FOLLOWING JESUS INTO THE THORNY PLACES

SHAYNE WHEELER

"SHAYNE HAS INDEED FOLLOWED JESUS INTO THE THORNY PLACES. BEFORE YOU FINISH THE FIRST CHAPTER YOU WILL BE INSPIRED TO DO THE SAME!"
ANDY STANLEY
NORTH POINT MINISTRIES

Jesus does some of his best work amid the briarpatches of life. He loves and guides people through the thorny thickets; he binds up their scrapes and wounds. And he invites you to join him in his healing journey through the sharp brambles. Welcome to *The Briarpatch Gospel*. It's all about creating a community in which people walk honestly through life's issues—even the darkest, most painful problems and questions—*together*. Unafraid. Like Jesus did.

Sounding a radical message of grace, Shayne Wheeler challenges you to discover your own (or your church's) briarpatch—the area where you feel afraid or unequipped to go. Because Jesus is waiting for you in the midst of life's thorns—all you need to do is venture in and meet him there.

CP0628